Bernie's Paris

Bernie's Paris

TRAVEL STORIES WITH LOVE

Linda Spalla

Photography by Bernard Verdier
Cover Photo by Peggy Bilbro

ISBN: 1523491159
ISBN 13: 9781523491155
Library of Congress Control Number: 2016912148
CreateSpace Independent Publishing Platform
North Charleston, South Carolina

If you are lucky enough to have lived in Paris as a young man, then wherever you go for the rest of your life, it stays with you, for Paris is a moveable feast.

Ernest Hemingway

Disclaimer

BERNIE'S PARIS—TRAVEL STORIES WITH LOVE covers an eleven-year span from 2004 to 2015. Restaurants, museums, events, and other special mentions may have changed over time. Shops may have gone out of business; restaurants may have closed their doors or gotten new names. Please forgive references that are no longer current. This is not an official travel guide but a book of the heart about traveling, living, and loving in Paris as we have experienced it.

What never changes is the magic which is Paris. That we guarantee!

Dedication

To Andrew, Avery, Carson, and James

For whom Paris memories await

Acknowledgements

⟡

I CAN BUY A NEW car in an hour, pick out a new pair of shoes in five minutes, and read a good book overnight. Fast is the adjective to best describe me—except in regard to writing this book. I have discovered that some creations need to stew and simmer a while to slowly evolve into their best version. And a while, in this case, has been two years. I've learned to be patient, to restrain my tendency for quickness, and to indulge in the fruit of editing.

Writers survive only because a village of people surround them with encouragement, support, constructive criticism, and resources during this process. I am deeply grateful to my village.

First, many thanks to my readers along the way who sifted through sections and versions of this book without telling me to stop writing.

Secondly, my thanks to Jeanie Thompson, Executive Director of the Alabama Writers' Forum, for her help in composing a query letter and content suggestions. She has made personal memories with us in Paris and has skin in the game.

A shout-out goes to my social media guru, Nona Perdue at SocialK Communications, who suggested the title and helped me build a social platform.

A special thanks to Jessica Swift of Swift Enterprises, Inc., for editing suggestions on arrangement, for demanding a touch of grace to my words, and for making me dig harder and deeper for more personal, descriptive stories. And to Ann Marie Martin for an additional, critical set of editing eyes. A lovely surprise happened in Paris this summer (2016) when our new-found, Parisian friend, Ann Jeanne, offered to edit the book for French spelling, grammar, and context. Thank you, Ann, for this act of gracious friendship. And to photographer, Peggy Bilbro, for shooting the cover photo, with much help and support from hubby, Jim. Lastly, much fondness to Richard Nahem who has given writing and photography advice and most of all, friendship, through our years in Paris.

The quotations in this book are from internet searches on various websites such as Pinterest, BrainyQuote, bartelby, Barlett's Quotations, Thinkexist, and Goodreads. They are sourced exactly as they were on the websites.

Finally, to Bernie for his patience in reading each chapter; for taking, selecting, and inserting all the photographs; and for expressing his opinions, knowing that I would likely overrule him! He stuck with me to the end, and now together we have a mutual treasure, our Paris legacy.

Table of Contents

Introduction

⌒

Travel is the great classroom—better than any book, movie, magazine, television program, video game, or internet site. It teaches us to stretch across and beyond our fences. More than ever, we need travel to help smooth out the jagged edges of our present world.

– LINDA SPALLA

IT WAS A CRISP, OCTOBER evening in 2003, and I wanted to sit in the safety of *801*, an intimate, upscale eatery in our Southern city of Huntsville, Alabama. As I ogled my flounder almondine, I was silently praying Bernie would just take me home, with no pressure to make love. Not tonight, please . . . I wasn't ready, not by a long shot. What would I say? So awkward, so out of practice.

You see, I had only been dating Bernie a few months, and I was still waiting on a burst of fireworks, a flurry of titillating chemistry. So far, no butterflies, no breathless anticipation, no racing pulse—at least not for me. What I did sense were plenty of damnable red flags prompting me to scream "Fire!" and run away—red flags like pets, politics, and parenting.

But, there was a solid presence about him which mysteriously had kept me from bolting.

After dinner, Bernie lifted his long-stemmed glass of cherry-red pinot noir and leaned in across the white linen tablecloth. Laying his gargantuan hand tenderly over mine, he said, "Hey, would you come with me to Paris for a couple of weeks? I'd love to show you my hometown."

I was stunned and speechless, not because I didn't know that he was French, but because a long, intimate trip with him was nowhere on my horizon. Talk about being on different wavelengths—I was worried about having sex, and he was suddenly asking me to go to Paris! He was moving much too quickly, and I pummeled him with questions.

"When would we go? For how long? How much would it cost? Where would we stay?"

Swirling the wine in his glass, Bernie calmly replied with a convincing grin, "Leave everything to me. I've got several hundred thousand free miles with Delta so we'll fly first class! I'll find us a great little hotel; we'll stay a week in Paris, then rent a car and drive through some of the countryside."

He was like a little boy—wide-eyed, breathlessly hopeful, and tapping his fingers in anticipation of my response.

After some considerable, inane babbling, I eventually just said "yes" since I couldn't think of a really good reason to turn down such a fabulous offer.

That was almost twelve years ago, and my life has not been the same since then. That's what this book is about—how a surprising love developed and grew through my time in Bernie's Paris. This memoir is not meant to be a travel guide, at least not officially so, but we hope it spurs you to find someone you love and plan a Paris fling. It doesn't matter your age. Just like with us, it's never too late!

But first, our sagas—who are we and how did we meet?

CHAPTER 1

The Beginning

Le Début

—♭

You put one foot out the door and the adventure begins.

– CAROL GILIOTT[1]

REPETITIVE HURT, BROKEN DREAMS, TWO divorces, single parenting, and a frantically successful career—that was my life. I was fifty-seven years old, retired, and pretty much a mess emotionally. But I was healthy and still attractive (at least according to friends who constantly tried to boost my spirits). The painful truth was that I had given up on finding anything close to lasting love—the kind that nurtures trust and friendship, that doesn't care about make-up and pretense, that forgives and snuggles, that permits the bitch to emerge once in a while.

I had decided that kind of love wasn't in the cards for me, and I was tired of giving relationships my all, thinking that something would be different—this time. I had been crying-all-night, deep-in-the-gut alone for thirty-five years, even while I was married. I figured that was enough. It was all I could take.

---

1 Carol writes the whimsical and mouthwatering blog "Paris Breakfasts" used with permission from Richard Nahem's daily blog, "Eye Prefer Paris."

Oh, I was not blameless—but nearly. The details are not important or appropriate, but it's enough to say that I found divorce and its aftermath much harder work than marriage. In fact, I believe if people knew how awful divorce was going to be, they'd never go through with it. I became cynical, depressed, and reclusive much of the time. I crafted a special box called motherhood where I tried to keep the crazies of my life at bay and managed to raise a son and a daughter amid all the cracks of my knotty life. I waylaid any sense of failure with "I did the best I could." Well, looking back, maybe I did and maybe I didn't. But that's another book.

I was not plain as in "plain Jane" but plain as in simple, conservative, basic, God-fearing, and terribly naïve, despite my fifty-seven years. My sweet Mama had taught me to always do the right things with a Southern graciousness which, of course, included being a great pretender. And that was what I had become. I had fooled the world! I was a hard worker, a success weaver, an inspiring speech-giver, an immaculate housekeeper, a frugal miser—having once in my life been jobless and homeless. In true Southern finesse, I could turn nothing into something elegant. The outside of me looked great; the inside was covered in scar tissue.

Only a few knew my secret.

I was a total failure at intimate relationships, and that reality shadowed my life. I had fallen off the happily-ever-after wagon when I was only twenty-two, newly married, and right out of college. Since then, the murkiness had enveloped me. I was missing a spot of joy, and oh, how I resented it. I had read all the self-help books, knew the drill about being alone versus being lonely, knew about taking lemons and making lemonade, knew about how smart women make stupid choices[2], *ad nauseum.* I had the T-shirt! Most didn't notice my grief, however, because of my signature smile and outward enthusiasm. I hid the hurt well; practice had made perfect.

I was known in my progressive, high-tech town as a tough, competitive businesswoman—a rags-to-riches, scrappy broad. Perhaps that in itself was what stood between me and men—too much success, too much self-confidence, too much material accomplishment. I was "that woman who used

---

2 A reference to the book of the same name by Dr. Connell Cowan, Random House, 1990.

to manage the TV station." From my Calloway golf clubs to my expensive Acura, I sensed that men took one look at my credentials and fled, thinking I would be high maintenance and expensive to keep happy.

Then in mid-2003, thanks to a mutual friend, I met Bernie. (I had never known a Bernie before—surely a hidden message!) To heighten the drama, this mutual friend was Bernie's boss at the time. She told him that I had just written a book on leadership and shared an accurate dose of my other credentials. Ugh! I found out later that Bernie took weeks to call me. He actually bought my book and read it first. When he finally got in touch, he was cordial, assertive in his radio-announcer voice, and maybe just a little nervous. The conversation lasted all of three minutes, and we arranged to meet for a glass of wine the following week at a local restaurant. The days before our rendezvous, I tried not to think about it, which made me think about it even more. I didn't hold out much hope because I had been here before.

The day finally came, and I was ready to get it behind me. As I approached the restaurant and parked my car, my stomach was churning with that awful blind-date angst. I was wearing a light-weight brown pantsuit appliqued with tiny orange and lime green beads and accented with a lime green shell top. I thought it was the perfect outfit to wear—not too showy, but not dowdy; casual and friendly. I learned later that Bernie hates lime green!

Since we had never laid eyes on each other, I had given him a physical description of myself—blonde, petite, late fifties. He stood, waved, and I hurried over to the bar booth he had already gotten for us. Trying hard to shed the business woman mold, I offered a flimsy handshake. We got through the awkward introductions, sat down, and began the usual round of first-date crossfire.

"So, I know where you work, but what do you do there?" I asked right out of the gate.

"Well, I've had two careers. Right now, I manage different defense contracts on the Arsenal, but I'm also retired from the Army."

"And how long were you in the Army?"

"Twenty-two years!"

"Wow, did you like it? What was your rank?"

"Well, of course, I liked it, or I wouldn't have stayed so long," Bernie chortled. "I retired as a lieutenant colonel."

Anything military was not my world, but I had sense enough to appreciate that lieutenant colonel was an impressive achievement.

Changing the subject, Bernie said enthusiastically, "I read your leadership book, and I liked it!"

"Really? Thank you! I'm glad you did. Most men would never admit that," I said with a shocked smile. Bernie didn't seem to understand my point.

"There were a couple of things I didn't agree with," he continued, "but overall, it was a great read."

Of course, I took the bait. "And what didn't you like?" I asked, armed and ready to defend my positions.

How funny that I have no memory of what his answer was!

We talked about our backgrounds, our children, our views on a few political issues (he was testing me), and pleasantly left the door open for future contact. Thankfully, it was not one of those catastrophes where I wanted to run out of the restaurant at a nauseous gallop, wondering "what in the world was *that* all about?"

But that initial encounter was not love at first sight either. My man-type had always been breathlessly handsome, dashing, sexy, and mysterious. This stereotype is exactly what had gotten me into two bad marriages, two divorces, and heart-breaking love affairs. Bernie was a nice-enough-looking man, but definitely didn't fit the parameters of my ideal guy. He was seven years older; he was not a *GQ* hunk; and oh, my God, he was French!! Bill O'Reilly had been telling us not to eat French fries and not to drink French champagne. The bastards hadn't even committed to helping us fight the Iraq war. What in the world did I want with this French radical?

I fought the relationship with a stubborn tenacity because I was hell-bent on getting the type of man I wanted—one I could fall passionately into lust with, pine after, work hard to win over, and then get dumped at the end. You get the sad picture, *oui*? Melodrama was my middle name.

This internal struggle lasted for weeks. My friends kept telling me that he didn't have to be Mr. Right on the outside. They hounded me to look at the inside, at his personality, life habits, and how he treated me. Deep down, a gnawing "something" kept pulling at me to hang on, test the waters, wait a while, and see what happened. He was so different from anyone I had ever dated, (duh!) and I failed to catch the significance of that. He was obviously intelligent and very polite; he had read my book and liked it; he had a kind demeanor, and he had come highly recommended by a friend. I started asking myself, "So, what's not to like about this guy?"

Did I mention that Bernie drove a candy-apple-red Corvette or that his exquisite French phrases captivated his listeners? Or that he, now a widower, had been happily married for thirty-one years to a lady held in high regard in our city as a fabulous violin teacher and member of the symphony? Did I mention that, because of a successful marriage, he understood how to be in a relationship, how to give unselfishly, how to cherish a woman? Or that he wasn't a playboy, that he managed his finances well, and that he wasn't a narcissist? Did I mention that he fell off the deep end for me with a sincere sweetness that I had never known? Or that at age sixty-four, he set out to learn the ridiculously difficult game of golf, only because he knew it was important to me?

He wooed me with love letters, sweet poetry, and those wonderful cards-for-no-reason which would melt anyone's heart. Suddenly, here was a man who wanted me more than I wanted him, and I had no idea how to execute inside that playbook. I was too blind (and stupid) to see that this Frenchman could be the gift I had been waiting for all my life.

Just as I had had my share of pain coupled with great success, so had Bernie. Bernard (said in French like *Bear-nar* without the *d*) was born in Paris to a mother from *Ile Saint-Louis*—the oldest and most original part of Paris—and to a father from Alsace. They divorced after World War II. Bernie was yanked from Paris at age ten by a new stepfather and transported first to Oklahoma, then to Kansas. He knew only two English phrases—**Tom Mix**, his mother's favorite silent movie cowboy—and **okay**. He was thrown into a school system that had no appreciation for a little French boy dressed in leggings and a beret. His first school years in America were miserable, except for a cousin who took him under her wing and became his great protector.

As you can imagine, Bernie struggled terribly with English but excelled in science and math because of the more advanced educational system in France. In his heart, he yearned for his biological father who was still in France, but at such a young age, Bernie had no control over his life. His mother had severed contact with the natural father, and slowly Bernie's French roots faded away. As children do, he acclimated, but not without some deep scars.

In his teenage years, Bernie had to work to have spending money and did everything from selling lamps in a department store to stocking shelves at a local drug store in Wichita. He slowly matured on American soil, embracing the structure of the Boy Scouts and ROTC. These gave him, he says, "a sense of belonging somewhere" which, of course, was the hole in his young life. In college, he linked up with two other guys to form a locally popular singing group called *The Triads*. They had gigs all the time and made some decent money—Bernie being the resonating bass voice. Slowly, slowly, he was finding his niche in America.

After graduating from college with a commission in the United States Army as a reserve second lieutenant, Bernie made perhaps the best decision of his life when he married his college sweetheart, Marilyn. Two weeks after their marriage, he was deployed to Berlin, Germany and then months later to Vietnam with the 101st Airborne Division. Though a very difficult time of his life, this laid the groundwork for his successful, twenty-two-year military career.

Typical of his sense of fair play and wise compassion, Bernie made this offer to Marilyn when he retired from the Army, "You have followed me all over the world. I'll follow you wherever you want to go." Having been stationed at Huntsville's Redstone Arsenal years ago, they returned with their son, James, and Bernie began a second, twenty-year career as a program manager for various defense contractors. He did well at every turn, using his smarts in the nuclear weapons field and developing the MLRS (Multiple Launch Rocket System). Always, throughout both careers, his fluent French was a great asset—whether in Vietnam, Cambodia, or at the Pentagon—as well as his other attributes of duty, loyalty, and respect for a job well done.

Let me be clear. Though extremely worldly and Parisian-born, Bernie is American through and through. He tears up when he hears the National

Anthem. He was a devoted, passionate soldier and defended our country during a very tough struggle. For twenty-two years, he did whatever the United States Army told him to do without complaint or resistance. And yet, during all that time, **his heart never left Paris.** Reuniting with his biological father in his late forties, Bernie realized that Paris and France were definitely still in his blood. His late-in-life goal became to spend time in his homeland and link up with the remaining members of his French family.

Then, an unexpected blip hit Bernie's radar screen. In the mid-nineties, his wife, Marilyn, developed cancer. Suddenly, the next phase of his life became that of caregiver, and I have no doubt that he was a wonderful one. He lost her in 1996 to a second bout of cancer, and in essence lost his life. She had been his world. After a too-soon, short-lived, second marriage, he discovered what I knew so well—a pit of grief and loneliness. Ironically, the stage was set for our fateful connection. Would you believe that during much of this phase of his life, Bernie lived about a mile from me? We never knew each other, but he jogged by my house almost every day. Incredible!

Back to 2003 and our story. Days became weeks, and weeks evolved into a couple of months of dating, moving steadily forward. We fell into the habit of going to dinner every evening, a tradition which has continued now for eleven years! I was totally comfortable introducing him to my group of friends. He was an immediate hit in social settings because he was such an easy conversationalist. Therefore, on that fall evening when he invited me to Paris, I was surprised but not frightened. When I said "yes," I had no idea what the next eleven years would mean to my life. Through our time in Paris, Bernie opened my eyes to a new world which has made me richly different. Much more on that in the last chapter. I fell in love not only with him but also with his French family, his language, his city, and his country.

Our relationship was like a slowly simmering tea kettle—it took a while for the whistling to start, at least for me. And it took Paris to put us where love could mellow and mature. The very element I had feared the most, the French connection, became the catalyst for deep love. Bernie is now my best friend. I call him my late-in-life gift. In Paris, we have shared discovery of site and self; we have faced intrigue and the unknown; we have uncovered daily serendipities and bridged cultural voids; we have argued and faced serious ill-nesses. We have seen the inside and the underside of each other. In these later years of our lives—after heartbreak, loneliness, failure, and despair—we have become the missing piece in each other's life quilt.

To unearth more of this unlikely story between a love-starved Southern belle and an over-eager, homesick Parisian, turn the page!

CHAPTER 2

The Early Years and Trust

Les Premières années et la confiance

**...you'll have to fall in love at least once in your
life, or Paris has failed to rub off on you.**

– E.A.BUCCHIANERI, *BRUSHSTROKES OF A GADFLY*

IMAGINE LEAVING FOR A TWO-WEEK jaunt to Paris with a guy you hardly knew.
That was suddenly my reality.

Two things were on my side: Bernie would want to make a good impres-
sion in his hometown, and the French language would not be an issue. Was I
crazy to do this after such a short courtship? Probably, but I'm a risk taker and
at this age decided, "What the heck?" I could be safe and bored at home, or I
could go to Paris and potentially have the time of my life. I had a solid travel
background, a good sense of independence, and plenty of self-confidence. If
things fell apart, I was certain I could take care of myself and find a way safely
back home.

A week before our departure day, I remember making a list of all of the
outfits I was packing down to the accessories—shoes, scarves, belts, and jewelry. Then I tried on every ensemble, trying to create my Parisian style, whatever that was. I even went online and searched for that year's latest fashions.

The end result was *four* suitcases! What's so hilarious now is how overdressed I was, and, in some cases, almost better dressed than the Parisians. They have a magical way of mixing and matching the same few basic articles in exquisite finesse. I still can't tie a scarf with their elegant flair.

Oh yes, I also packed paper towels, napkins, coffee filters, and cleaning supplies— to which Bernie responded that we weren't going to a third-world country. "Yes, I know that," I said, but packed them anyway. It sounds pretty ridiculous now. I do still take a fold-up clothes hamper for going to the laundry, ice-cube trays, face cloths, spices, and a kit of household items like paper clips, scissors, Scotch tape, and bag clips. Bernie takes note pads, envelopes, batteries, and all the connectivity like converters and adapters. We both have our stuff! And make note that we usually stay for two months!

(On that first trip and even now, Bernie takes *one* large suitcase plus a small carry-on. I dare him to say a word. I cannot go to Paris with one pair of shoes as he does and one tiny zipper bag of toiletries! Men have to learn how to travel successfully with their women. Don't tell us how to pack. Simply accept that we'll do it our way, and life will be much better!)

We flew Delta First Class on Bernie's leftover business miles, and it was perfect—French food, plenty of wine, and reclining seats. Bernie was sweet, attentive, and excited, holding my hand most of the time. The flight attendant labeled us "two love birds."

A favorite moment was seeing the Eiffel Tower for the first time on our landing approach at *Charles de Gaulle* airport and gasping at its breathtaking beauty. This massive yet delicate structure was towering over Paris like a graceful piece of latticework, sparkling in the early-morning sunshine. Perhaps Kristin Harmel says it best in *The Sweetness of Forgetting,* "I've seen it in photographs a thousand times, but seeing it in person for the first time, that reminds me that I'm really, truly here, thousands of miles away, across an ocean from home." I could definitely relate to that feeling. It was a heady moment. Despite the fact that my body was exhausted from the seven-hour flight, despite my upside-down body clock, I couldn't wait to get off the plane and start the adventure!

Knowing only two French words, *bonjour* (hello) and *oui* (yes), I had no idea what to expect. I exited the plane and came face to face with the large sign reading *Bienvenue* (Welcome). This would prove to be a harbinger for my experience with Paris —I have never felt anything but welcome. Going through customs was a breeze, and then we were off to baggage claim.

We took a taxi to our pre-booked hotel in the Latin Quarter and stored our luggage. (Most hotels in Paris have a check-in time of three o'clock in the afternoon. If you arrive earlier, they will usually provide a secure spot for luggage storage.) Then we sprinted off to the *Métro* which would shuttle us around Paris for the day. I got my first lesson from Bernie, who was an expert. He carefully pointed out *la correspondance* (the change from one line to another) and *sortie*, the exit.

Our first stop was the Eiffel Tower. However, when I saw the hordes of people queued up under its four massive feet, I protested loudly.

"Bernie, are you sure we want to stand in this long line? Look at all the people and all the kids! It's going to take hours."

"Oh, it's okay. The line will move quickly. You'll see. Look at the marvelous elevators! They are over a hundred years old."

"Who cares about the darn elevators?" I thought to myself, not wanting to be rude. We spent over two hours waiting to go up to the top with hundreds of other people. Once there, we lingered for quite a while basking in the breath-taking view—the River *Seine* bending like a graceful lady through the city, the broad avenues embracing the ancient structures in perfect symmetry, and the people far below swarming like tiny ants at a picnic. I was sorry that I had whined about the long wait! It was my first gasp at the beauty of Paris.

We ate a bite of very late lunch across *Le Trocadéro* or huge plaza in front of the Tower. Then it was back to the *Métro* for the return to our hotel. We arrived just before six o'clock, only to find that our late reappearance meant a slightly inferior room. We made do in a tiny space in this very three-star hotel and had dinner at a crazy nook called *Le Coupe-Chou*, hidden in an alleyway down from the Pantheon. As we've since learned, it's a Parisian treasure, but that first night, I had the worst piece of chicken I had ever eaten, a fried chicken leg that was scrawny and covered with tough, thick, fatty skin. My immediate thought was, "What in the world have I gotten myself into?"

Arriving at nine, taking a taxi to the hotel for luggage storage, then the *Métro* to the Eiffel Tower, eating a late lunch (almost always two hours), and returning late in the afternoon taught us a lesson. Moving around in Paris is time-consuming. Most first-timers pack too much into their day and then get frustrated and maybe even agitated with each other. Allow for plenty of travel time and unexpected delays. Keep your schedule flexible so you won't negate the fun of exploring together.

Bernie was a superb host on this initial trip. He was patient, tolerant, and answered all of my questions about the *Métro*, the menu, and the cultural differences. He was truly in his element.

"Look," he said, as he pointed up to the street numbers on our first time out, "The numbers are not consistent like ours and sometimes out of order. Some façades don't even have a number; you have to be careful and keep looking. Forget about odd on one side of the street and even on the other. It's pretty confusing!"

Also, though I craved coffee with dessert, he explained,

"That's a no-no in Paris; dessert first, and then coffee. You'll get used to it!"

It was dozens of small details that were foreign to me, and he smoothed them out like silky powder on a baby's bottom.

That first week overwhelmed me with a deluge of stimuli, trying to see everything as though we were never coming back. We zipped around to *Le Louvre, Le Musée d'Orsay, l'Avenue des Champs Elysées, Sainte-Chapelle, Notre Dame,* and the River *Seine.* My memories are fuzzy from ten years ago, but I do remember walking hand in hand along the *Seine* in a darkening twilight and thinking that surely this must be a dream. It was story-book romantic, and I was warming to the fact that Bernie was dear to have brought me to his home town. I will always cherish that walk and call it forward in my memory every year as we stroll along the same path.

Another unexpected sensation during that first week was acclimating to the ***smell*** of Paris. How do I describe it? It's a combination of bread baking, car exhaust fumes, a bit of sewer gas, potatoes frying, cigarette smoke, and musty sea water. Sounds pretty gross, I know, but it isn't! It is a distinctive smell, the very essence of Paris. If you've been there, you will no doubt recognize my description. It becomes comfortably familiar, like the scent of your favorite grandmother's living room as you step into her house.

Our second week, we rented a car and started a jaunt through the *Loire* Valley. What an experience! Bernie drove first, and I gritted my teeth as he fought with the straight transmission, trying to shift gears in a strange car. That led to a conversation on motion sickness, and my pleading with him not to swerve and jerk the car! There was no cruise control function, which only made matters worse. I fought to survive the jerky ride and then tried my hand at driving, only to be flustered with the road signs, speed limits, traffic circles (roundabouts), and the darn motorcycles whizzing *between* lanes on the interstates, almost clipping the side mirrors!

(Here's some helpful info for those courageous enough to drive in France. French roads, though well-marked, have a confusing system of maps identifying regional, city, or national routes. The principle is similar to ours, but it takes a while to figure out how to match the road signs with the maps which, of course, you don't want to do while driving! Watch out for the hidden, roadside cameras. It doesn't matter that you're in a rental car. In 2015, Bernie got a months-old speeding ticket in his mailbox from the French government!)

On this off-road trip, I remember beautiful *châteaux* and interesting hotel rooms, coupled with lugging suitcases in and out of our small Renault as we slept in a different bed every night. I remember finding the tiny villages and road network that supported them absolutely fascinating. I learned quickly that the secret to driving out in rural areas like this was knowing what your next little hamlet was, **not** the big city you were heading to for the night. We kept yellow sticky notes on the dashboard, and we did all of this without a GPS! Getting a little lost was totally part of the experience, and highly recommended.

My biggest difficulty early on was the food—so strange. So unsure of what I had just ordered, many times I would leave the food uneaten, a terrible *faux pas* (misstep) in France. Or I would trade with Bernie if he had something that looked better. He was good-natured about that, but must have gotten aggravated with me. Over the years, I have developed a thorough understanding of food terms and menu selections—in French—but I still have a set of what I call "safe foods" when I'm in doubt. These include an omelet, *pommes frites* (French fries), club sandwich, Caesar salad with chicken, *foie gras* (goose liver), any kind of *crêpe*, and almost any dessert. I can survive! I don't order beef; Bernie thinks I'm crazy. Hamburgers, maybe; but regular steaks, no. They are cut and cooked differently from the American way. You can try them and see what you think.

In reflecting back, I had no appreciation for the language. I stayed confused and isolated from any communication except with Bernie. Embarrassed, shy, and afraid to open my mouth, I walked around in a fog using Bernie as my headlights. I couldn't even watch television. My advice would be to learn some French phrases before you go. Either pull out your high-school French book or invest in a program like Rosetta Stone or Duolingo and start learning conversational French. I've gone through Rosetta multiple times. French is a language you sing, not say; and even now, my Alabama accent makes it doubly difficult. The point is that I keep trying!

Our second year's visit to Paris brought some ease and familiarity. I carefully whittled down to three large suitcases, still too many by Bernie's standards. I figured out a little about wardrobe, especially shoes which are heavy and quickly add to the fifty-pound suitcase limit. (I have learned to put them in my carry on.) That year, I took no paper towels so there was some progress!

We stayed in a different hotel which was close to *Le Palais Royal* (The Royal Palace) with Bernie's former boss, Jan, who introduced us, and her companion, Tony. It was a perfect location, and we spent two weeks in the city retracing some of our steps. The highlights of that trip were a lunch at *Jules Verne* in the Eiffel Tower (which was our first encounter with exquisite French dining in a starred restaurant) and an evening at *Le Moulin Rouge*, thanks to the generosity of our friends in both cases.

I'm ashamed to say that in this second jaunt to Paris, I still had no appreciation for the language and no desire to learn it. I made progress with the food, but ever so slowly. Those first two years, there was no blog or daily communication with friends back home. Our trip was still just a visit and not a residence.

Bernie was learning about my many quirks; I was learning about his, and he worked hard to keep me happy. We were ever so slowly finding our special

Parisian cadence. I was discovering why Bernie felt a tender fondness for Paris and was finding him more and more attractive in this environment. I loved the history, the architecture, the frenzy of big city life, the *Métro*, the strolling, the ancient streets. He was ecstatic that I was starting a love affair with his hometown, and we both saw the potential to enjoy many future visits here together. As I absorbed French culture, I began to see a light opening inside me, an aperture to acceptance and tolerance that I had never experienced.

We were at our best in Paris—Bernie, definitely the alpha dog, and I, the loyal companion, following along beside him. Now really—what man doesn't like that?

Purely Paris tips for a first visit

- **Pack something overtly orange...purse, gloves, scarf, socks. If you want to really be Parisian, your scarf should never match anything else you are wearing.**

- **Check out an all-French airline called *La Compagnie*. Not only are the planes new, but the seats make into beds at the push of a button. The French food and service are impeccable. And the ticket prices are unbeatable, around $2000, round trip, per person. However, it flies only out of Newark, New Jersey, and has no luggage transfer with the other airlines.**

- **Don't buy euros in America! During your trip, use your bank debit or credit card, even when you first arrive at the airport. Know all of your PINs. Research the fees for each of your cards and ascertain which is best for ATM withdrawals and which for charges. Don't think you can walk into a bank in Paris. They exist for their own customers; the entrances have keypads with personalized codes so you will not be able to get inside to change money. NEVER use a money-changing store. We've done all of this the wrong way, like making a spectacle of ourselves trying to get into a bank. You name it; we've tried it. So trust our experience on this one. The ATM in French** is *le distributeur de billet,* and they are around every corner and at both airports. By the way, be sure to notify your credit card companies and your bank of your travel dates.

- If you are staying in Paris for seven days or less, here's a tip to decrease jet lag. Make changes to your sleep patterns before you leave. Seven days out, start going to bed one hour earlier and getting up one hour earlier each day. By the time you leave, you will be going to bed about six o'clock in the evening and getting up at one or two o'clock in the morning. Then, during your flight over, SLEEP at least five hours, even if you have to take a sleeping pill. Drink lots of water, and when you arrive, your body clock will <u>almost</u> be attuned to local time. Do NOT take a nap your first day in Paris as that will negate all of your preparation.

- Pack your own face cloths for your shower or bath because you will likely find none in your apartment or hotel. The best you may have are small hand mittens.

- It's best not to come to Paris for your one trip of a lifetime during the month of August. Many stores and restaurants are closed, and many Parisians are out of the city. And it's hot, hot, hot with very little air conditioning. April through July are the ideal months. September and October can be nice if you don't mind shorter days, and we understand the lights at Christmas are lovely if you can endure the cold, rainy weather.

- Bring good, but not new walking shoes, and then buy some great Parisian shoes for fancy *soirées* after you arrive. I suggest that you throw away the pair of shoes that have walked all the many Parisian miles because they will get dirty, wet, and worn. This will make room for the new pair in your suitcase!

CHAPTER 3

Finding an Apartment in Paris

Trouver un appartement à Paris

⎯⎯⎯

*There are only two places in the world where we
can live happy: at home and in Paris.*

– ERNEST HEMINGWAY

ON OUR THIRD TRIP TO Paris, Bernie wanted to stay much longer. He was not
content to **visit**; he wanted to **live** for a while in his hometown. And a while
became two months! I freaked out at first but was determined to prove both to
myself and to him that I could do it. The thought of shutting down my life—
walking away from board commitments and meetings, leaving my kids and
grandkids, unravelling my daily routine—caused me to catch my breath and
feel slightly nauseated. There were so many details to address like stopping
mail, moving plants, setting up online bill paying, stopping the newspaper,
getting medicines, knowing passwords. Yikes!

Saying goodbye to girlfriends who were my mainstay was hard until one
pulled me up by my bootstraps and chided,

"Girlfriend, you're getting to spend two months in Paris! The rest of us
are green with envy."

Perspective gained.

To clarify, Bernie lopes along through life like a happy kid licking his ice cream cone, and I run a frantic maze of details like a crazed rat. Opposites do attract. I call it our "speeds." I'm in fast speed most of the time—organizing, culling, rearranging, preparing, and divesting life of much of its spontaneity. Bernie is in slow speed—relaxed, unbothered, and always ready to enjoy a glass of wine or two or three.

Paris has moved both of us slightly more to the middle and into each other's turf. I've learned to slow down and relax, and Bernie has accepted that we do need some structure and planning to make the best of our time. The middle is a darn good place to be.

Despite our differences, we worked together to find a suitable place to stay, and we spent hours and hours researching Paris apartments on the internet. How did we function before the marvel of bringing our world so close to us? Some might argue that the internet has taken the mystery and surprise out of travel. *Au contraire!* I would protest loudly that it has provided predictability and sanity to our travels.

There are many good websites for apartment hunting, depending on your available budget, but initially, we found one of the best to be *www.paristay.com*. It's an easy site to navigate with a clever system of icons which represent all the amenities in the apartment. This site also provides thirty to thirty-five photographs of the interior along with great descriptions, room by room, and a summary of the surrounding area. Just be advised that there is an agency fee of fifteen percent of your total rent added to your final charge if you use this site (and most others), and you will probably have to put down a refundable deposit, pre-pay at least half of the rent, and sign a contract. Yes, it's a bit cumbersome and scary, but after a time or two, you will get the hang of it.

There are other good websites, some hosted by owners, as well as home swaps. Check out all of them to find what works best for you. Some are cheaper, but be careful. The one apartment we rented in Cannes directly from an owner for a great price left me with bedbug bites! The professional websites overseen by an agency seem to insure higher standards.

Don't be afraid to try to negotiate the price; however, it may take getting to know your landlord or lady to make this happen. It's France, and polite relationships make all the difference. Now, in our second apartment, we get a remarkable deal because we have become good friends with the landlady and her family.

It helps at the start of your search if you know how Paris is arranged and where you want to stay; otherwise, any of the web sites will be confusing. Spend some time with a city map. Paris is divided into twenty *arrondissements* or districts, each of which has its own city hall and mayor. The first four *arrondissements* represent old Paris. The fifth through the twentieth flow in clock-wise circles from the center.

The cost of your apartment will be determined by the *arrondissement* you select. The most elite areas are around the Eiffel Tower (known as the 7th"), on *Ile Saint-Louis* (the 4th) and in the 16th and 17th *arrondissements*. An apartment along *l'Avenue des Champs Elysées* (the 8th) would be three times what we are accustomed to paying. We live like middle class citizens in Paris; we have what we need, but it's certainly not the Ritz. We think you have a more authentic Parisian experience if you don't go too high end.

If I was going to **live** in Paris for two months, I had many questions. Unlike Bernie, who can sleep on a flagpole and be happy in a tent, I needed some creature comforts. I wanted to know—did we have an internet connection, a coffee pot, a dishwasher, a washing machine, a telephone? Were pets allowed before us? Hopefully not. Was smoking allowed? Again, hopefully not. What floor were we on? What subway station were we near? What did the neighborhood look like, and what shops were nearby? How many square feet were we living in, one floor or two, how many bathrooms, how much closet space? You get the picture! All of these impact the quality of a visit for me, the crazed rat. Bernie was patient, and we made a mutually good choice. We've mastered this process over time and know exactly *where* to look, what to look *for* and what to look *out* for. There's a difference.

We narrowed the search to a dozen choices, began a spreadsheet comparison, and finally, agreed on an apartment at *92 rue Saint-Antoine* in *Le Marais* which is the 4th *arrondissement.* The owner was a British author who used the flat occasionally as a writing studio.

When we arrived that warm summer day to our bright blue, street-front doorway, we punched in the security code, went racing up the wide, marble, circular stairway, opened the cream-colored door, and hit a wall of reality.

"Oh, my gosh, Bernie! This is so much smaller than it looked on the internet. What happened?" I asked in shock as we inched inside.

"Hmm," Bernie said as he slowly walked around. With a disappointing tone, he said, "What happened is a wide-angle lens! It *is* very small, and where the hell is the second bathroom? I know there was a water closet on the first floor."

"Look! Why are there towels in the washing machine? How strange!" I said, reaching to open the door.

"Oh, my God, Bernie! The door handle is missing—I mean totally missing. What do you think happened?"

"Well, I guess the renters before us tried to force the door open and broke off the handle. That's a problem!"

"Do ya think?" I said in horror. "This means we have no washing machine and no towels to use in the meantime." I raced upstairs to look for additional towels. Of course, there were none. (By the way, in Paris, generally the washer and dryer are combined in one machine, and the dryer cycle is not worth a flip!)

Bernie followed me upstairs and had to tilt his shoulders sideways to even get up the narrow staircase. The bathroom sink was inside the bedroom, and the shower and toilet had only a sliding glass door for privacy. The only closet was so teensy that we foresaw having to stuff our clothes inside, and I realized right away that I'd have to use the stairway bannister frame for things like scarves, belts, jackets, and pajamas. There was nothing like a chest of drawers. The bed was pushed totally against one wall so Bernie had to crawl across to get in. (Who's thinking about sex now?!) The sink had no counter space for any of our toiletries—okay for Bernie with his tiny toiletry case but disastrous for me with my two dozen bottles, jars, hairdryer, hot comb, hairspray, you name it!

The living room, eating area, and kitchen were all one room. The best part of the apartment was the bright red and chrome kitchen. Yes, no misprint—bright red appliances and cabinet facades, very modern and high quality. We had scads of kitchen cabinet space, but little space to relax, read a book, or take a quick nap. I'm not a fancy cook so the joke was on me! We pushed our suitcases under the Plexiglas dining room table—more like a card table—which meant that our knees were jammed up against the table legs when we sat down. The television consumed one end of the table, but at least, most of the channels were in English, thanks to our British landlady.

Eventually, after the initial entry shock, we heard a knock at the door, and opened it to a young woman from the rental agency. She was there to greet us, give us more keys, and relay the bad news about the broken washing machine. She confirmed that the previous renters had angrily tried to force the door open before the "unlock" light had come on. The door handle had snapped off, and she made it very clear that this was a big, ugly no-no!

In typical American fashion, I protested vigorously and not very politely that we had paid to have a functional washing machine, to which she curtly replied,

"I'm very sorry, but this is Paris. Nothing here is easy like in America, and it will probably be two weeks before we can get a service rep from Darty (like our Westinghouse) to come fix the problem."

That was my baptism in how **not** to be rude to the French and how to embrace the all-too-frequent phrase that is part of Parisian life—it's complicated.

One of the funniest stories in this first apartment happened midway through our stay. I had tied up all the rubbish in one large plastic bag and set it outside the front door, so I wouldn't forget to take it downstairs. Shortly, there was a loud, aggressive rap at the front door. I opened it to a sophisticated and smartly dressed French madam who was definitely not happy. She snipped that she was a medical doctor with an office on the floor above us and would certainly appreciate my not littering the stairway! It was a lesson in French culture, and I never did that again!

Was the first time as an apartment dweller totally happy? The simple answer is "no." I got a little homesick, lonely, and hated the dreary rainy days. Bernie simmered along better than I, though we were both very disappointed in the size and inconvenience of the apartment. We made it work because we had no choice. Unlike today, I didn't venture out much on my own. Intimidated by the newness, the strange nuances of French culture, and the absence of luxuries, I was a spoiled American! Ah, but the memory of that first apartment stay is definitely a warm fuzzy! We've had eight more years in *Le Marais*, home to some of the most eclectic boutiques, some of the oldest buildings, and also the historic Jewish district. And every year, we can't wait to get back because we discover new streets, serendipities, strolls, and thrills to delight us.

Good luck on selecting the right apartment for you and your budget. It's out there with some persistent research, and it's the only way to truly experience Paris. *Très bien!* (Very good!)

Purely Paris:

Apartment living in Paris is not perfect. I once temporarily lost a $4,000 rent payment to a management group that went bankrupt. Citi, my credit card bank, resolved the dispute in my favor but not without a few scary weeks! Beware of anyone who asks for full payment up front. I should have known better.

CHAPTER 4

Making Your Apartment Work in Paris

L'Appartement—ça marche; ça ne marche pas

Whoever does not visit Paris regularly will never really be elegant.

– HONORÉ DE BALZAC

OUR SECOND APARTMENT AT *42 rue Saint-Paul* has become our Paris nest. It's a fascinating step back into the sixteenth century. Imagine, living in a building from the 1500s! The walls are a foot thick, and the ceilings are reinforced with massive wooden beams—think Tudor! Though it has been completely remodeled, the apartment is, of course, constricted by the building's age. Thus, there is no central heat and air, only fans for the summer and electric radiators for winter; and just to retrofit the plumbing must have been a construction feat.

L'appartement à Paris is the ultimate cultural immersion. Bernie and I had no idea how this might affect our relationship, since we live separately in Alabama. Suddenly, we found ourselves at a defining crossroads: exploring the newness together, and disrupting the familiar together. How we reacted outside our comfort zones could have created some potential explosions; we stayed cognizant of the stress points and made sure our relationship didn't come unglued!

I wanted desperately to acclimate, to accept, and to fall into the Parisian groove—I truly, truly did! But I pined silently for an ice dispenser in the refrigerator door, Press 'N Seal in the pantry, *NCIS* on the television, and something besides a hand-held shower sprayer, *sans* a shower curtain. At different moments, I felt resentment, anger, and fear—resentment, because I didn't know it would be like this; anger, because none of the oddities seemed to bother Bernie, and fear, because I didn't have my usual sense of control. I was at the mercy of the apartment and its quirks, and of Bernie to guide me through them.

I was "the lady with no clothes"—my vulnerability and lack of control were exposed as though I were standing naked before the whole city. I couldn't speak to anyone, didn't know anyone, and didn't understand how things functioned. It was a raw, overwhelming feeling. But it didn't last long! As I said before, we found a rhythm that worked for us, soon doing the Paris two-step together—light, airy, spontaneous, and downright fun, which is the beauty of an elongated stay.

Bernie frequently says that I'm prone to be a doom-and-gloom person. He will grab me by the shoulders, put us nose to nose, and say, "Just chill out!"

That, of course, makes me even more tense, and my protective response is, "I am **not** a pessimist; I'm a realist!"

And then we're off into that world of couple friction with jibs and jabs that up stress levels and raise blood pressures. I see the potential for disaster and try to plan against it. Bernie plows ahead without worry or concern and makes the best of any situation. Though I try to be more like him, I'm simply not. So, we do have our moments, and **none is touchier than when we enter a new apartment.**

I am a quick study and see the potholes in our new surroundings long before Bernie does. With one visual sweep of each room, I see what's clean and what's not—fingerprints on the glass tables, dust on the window sills, dirty baseboards. I see what's going to work and what's not—the small pantry stuffed with clutter, no place for suitcase storage, an absence of closet hangers. I see what's going to fit and what's not—the useless tea kettle on the kitchen counter taking up one of the precious-few electrical outlets or artsy items that need moving to make way for essentials. I've learned to speak less, listen more, and withhold my caustic judgments because it only infuriates Bernie and validates his belief that I'm a pessimist. It's a tangle of words and emotions I try to leave at the curb. I process in silence to keep the peace, and then, you guessed it, I quietly do what I want to make the apartment more to my liking!

One inevitable challenge that comes with apartment living will be steps—many, many steps. If you are limited at all physically, pay close attention to which floor your prospective apartment is on when you book it, and whether it has a lift (elevator). The steps are great exercise from day to day but very demanding when you are moving in and out. Hauling heavy suitcases up and down narrow steps and circular stairways is treacherous and will most assuredly give you incentive to pack lighter. We navigate thirty-four steps up and thirty-four steps down every time we enter and leave. (Sometimes if our regular apartment is not available during our dates, we have secured other apartments, one with seventy-eight steps in each direction!)

Another challenge will be street noise. If your apartment is on a busy corner like ours, then you'll want to be a few floors up or on the inside of a courtyard. My remedy is to use ear plugs at night. I purchase the smaller ones designed for women; otherwise, I would never fall asleep. The noises of the night continue until two and three o'clock in the morning, and sometimes, on holiday *fêtes* will persist until dawn.

Another issue may be closet space, which might be non-existent or minimal at best. We push suitcases behind chairs and sofas, under staircases, wherever there's any space at all. We use them for storing purchases bought throughout the trip to keep clutter to a minimum. We use stair banisters for hanging articles of clothing and have purchased behind-the-door hooks for towels, coats, bathmats, or scarves. Those that fit over the door are best. Since we generally get the same apartment, we have enjoyed these investments year after year—our landlady indulges us and lets them remain. Bernie has taken a hanging, closet-storage rack made of fabric that was already in the apartment and reinforced it with wooden slats that he found on the street from fruit vendors! It made the shelves much sturdier and kept the entire apparatus from imploding. It's an artistic piece!

Paris apartments have 220 electricity as opposed to 110. Take converters *and* adapters with you—just the adapter alone will burn up your appliance. All it does is make the plug fit into the outlet. The converter converts the current. Who knew? Of course, Bernie did. I default all things electrical and technical to him. If your apartment has its own computer, expect a different, crazy keyboard which will surely drive you nuts. Many of the keys are in different places from our QWERTY keyboard, including all the French accent symbols. You'll get used to it, or take your own iPad as I do— lightweight and works on European current with a plug adapter. Absolutely, make sure you have Wi-Fi in the apartment. Otherwise, you'll have to take your own router, and that gets <u>extremely complicated</u>. Just ask Bernie how many hours he's worked on router issues, prior to our having Wi-Fi. It was the answer to our technical problems in the last several visits. By the way, here's a funny for you. In Paris, Wi-Fi is pronounced as Wee-Fee. We get some interesting looks when we return to the States and refer to Wee-Fee out in public.

Good lighting will probably be another issue. Plan to purchase some extension cords, and do a little redecorating with light. Electrical outlets are few and often inconveniently located. The lamps are more about artistic style than good lighting, in my opinion. If you're a reader, hopefully you'll have your digital books downloaded on your Kindle, Nook, or iPad. Or if you're old-school, take a book light for bedtime reading.

Having Bernie around in our apartment is such a blessing. He can truly do anything and *has* during our stays on *rue Saint-Paul*. He has fixed the dishwasher, glued down a slat in the hardwood floor, creatively strengthened the closet hanger I just described, and rigged up all manner of conveniences for company who have stayed with us. There's no electricity in the guest bathroom, and he has a system of extension cords that are intricate and amazing. He's a mechanical genius.

Our apartment on *rue Saint-Paul*

I, on the other hand, maintain the kitchen to my liking and keep the floors mopped and dusted. We both participate in the laundry, and Bernie always does the vacuuming—the bags never get changed, it seems, except by him. Dust from the outside settles quickly, black dust from car fumes. I bring my trusty Swifter duster mop that comes apart in four sections and a hand duster, though you can purchase these in Paris now.

As to appliances, our dishwasher is half the size of what we have at home, but it works remarkably well. However, Paris water, though completely drinkable, is high in calcium. I purchase the most expensive dishwashing detergent that has anti-calc additives, or our dishes come out milky and spotted. Our microwave works quite well but is missing the familiar panel of numbers for entering the cook time. There's one knob that turns to thirty seconds, one minute, two minutes—then a start button. I forget from year to year how this crazy set-up works. The refrigerator is very large for Paris but has a tiny freezer, acceptable because of daily shopping. If you like ice, bring your own plastic ice trays. We've gone through several as they seem to get thrown away. I pack them now if I have room. The TSA loves it!

Initially, the queen bed in our apartment was low to the floor and hard, an issue that even got the best of Bernie. It was like sleeping on bricks, and for a couple of years, it was enough to give us pause to find a different apartment. The pillows had no fluff at all. We've run the gamut of using an air mattress to letting our displeasure be known to a neighbor. This circulated back to our thoughtful landlady, and eventually, we were surprised with a wonderful, new mattress and new pillows!

Changing a bed is hilarious. Parisians use a huge down comforter around which a big sheet fits. It serves as your top sheet AND your bed-spread, thus the need to wash it frequently. It has about an 18-inch slit in the bottom into which (after it's washed) you have to stuff the huge down monstrosity. It's actually the funniest thing we do, like fighting a bear, which results in finally just laughing our way through it! Just a top sheet and a separate comforter would be SO much easier. I'm sure there's a system we don't know.

The secret to loving *chez* Bernie and Linda (our house) is interacting with the neighbors. We have loved getting to know them and have get-togethers several times during our stay. Above us is a French couple with two children. Bearded, burly Frank is a hard-working artist who creates amazing *objets d'art* out of recycled items—pieces like lamps and robots, and he hosts expositions around the city to showcase and sell his works. He speaks good English, loves his champagne, and loves talking politics. He grew up in this apartment which he now occupies with his wife and children, but has done significant remodeling. Like Bernie, he can do anything! His last project was putting in a totally new kitchen. His wife, Vinciane, is so very French—tiny, elegant, and chic. Initially, she was very shy about speaking English around us but has improved greatly. They decided to take part of their large apartment and convert it to a rental. Frank did all the renovation and together they manage the bookings, the cleaning, and much of the hospitality. It has been extremely successful. We have watched their son, Celestin, grow from a baby to now eight years old, and little Alice, the daughter, is four. They are a precious family and great neighbors who helped us out of a very tight spot once. More about that in chapter seventeen when we describe our worst trip ever!

We adore our other neighbor, Chantal, whose apartment is on the same floor as ours. A native Parisian, she is a retired UNESCO employee, speaks fantastic English and delightfully expressive French, and is brimming over with charming stories about her exotic, world travels. She wistfully describes the Paris of her youth and sadly thinks the culture has diminished through the decades. Chantal is plugged into the Paris arts community and is an artist herself, focusing on Japanese paintings. She tends a lovely array of house plants just outside our front door, making us feel right at home. We now exchange Christmas cards every year.

We've even made acquaintance with the concierge who mops the hallways and steps, as well as with the hairdresser downstairs and an entrepreneur named Patrick who owns a little café, just steps from the entrance to our building. The point is that on any given day, we can walk up and down our area and say *Bonjour* to our friends. To Bernie, this is heaven!

We take exceptionally good care of the apartment, almost a pride of ownership! One year, someone had sprayed red paint across the security keypad at the street entrance. Highly offended, I used fingernail polish remover and a Q-Tip on it. *Voilà,* it disappeared!

If you choose the apartment route, the surrounding area will soon become familiar. Like us, you will set your clock by the church bells; you will listen for the police whistles and the mounted Republican Guard, clip-clopping by on horseback outside your window. You will be saying *Bonjour* to the proprietors, the fruit vendors, the hairdressers, and even the homeless people you see every day. With time, you will forget about the aggravations and inconveniences and embrace this simpler, enjoyable lifestyle. Paris will get into your bloodstream almost before you know it! *Tout marche*! (Everything works!)

Purely Paris

42 Bis Rue Saint-Paul

Looking for something affordable in Paris other than a hotel? Want the absolute authentic Parisian experience in daily living? We've got the place for you. It's actually one floor above our apartment and is owned by Frank and Vinciane, our neighbors. They turned half of their top-floor apartment into a delightful efficiency space they rent out very affordably. It has a private entrance, kitchenette, eating bar, and all-new bathroom. It's fully equipped with coffee pot, microwave, dishes, and glassware. It's probably not more than two hundred and fifty square feet and will accommodate only two people. The only drawback—four flights of steps! For more information, google *https://www. airbnb.fr/rooms/878992.*

CHAPTER 5

Daily Living in Paris

La Vie quotidienne à Paris

There is but one Paris and however hard living may be here,
and if it became worse and harder even—the French air
clears up the brain and does good—a world of good.

— Vincent van Gogh

LES JOURNÉES (THE DAYS)

As APARTMENT DWELLERS, WE SETTLED into daily life in Paris in the heart of
the *Marais* district—the 4th *arrondissement*.

I had no clue where we were, no idea what *Le Marais* was, or how to get
around. I didn't know it had been a swamp hundreds of years ago or that,
later in the sixteenth century, it became home to the kings of France. I was
glued to Bernie's hip and never ventured out by myself. I didn't know that we
were only two blocks from the river or on the major thoroughfare that led to
the *Louvre*, or that we were three blocks from *La Place de la Bastille* or near
one of the loveliest parks in Paris, *La Place des Vosges*. It was a charming area,
but I had no idea then what a great chance selection we had made in terms
of location. Coincidentally, the wonderful apartment that we have grown to
love on *rue Saint-Paul* is right across the street from that tiny nook with the
red kitchen!

Our first outing was to the grocery store; then, we oriented ourselves in terms of the subway station, some shops, *la boulangerie* (bakery), pharmacy, restaurants, and cafés. We were right next to a fire station, which meant screaming sirens at all hours of the day and night, but offered a consoling sense of security in case of an emergency. Shopping, even in the grocery store, was tough the first time. Despite the great variety, the brands and logos were foreign to me. I remember standing in bewilderment in front of the coffee aisle looking at dozens of labels. An older French lady, probably in her seventies and dressed in black, tapped me on the shoulder, obviously sensing my confusion. She pointed to the brand called *Carte Noir* and with her kind eyes and gestures assured me that this was the best choice. It's the coffee I still buy, and it's **wonderful**—rich, bold, Arabica.

The unwritten manual for daily living was an enigma—how to order, what to say, where to try on, how to pay, how to greet. I felt like a fumbling novice. However, I soon learned that the French are very forgiving. The cashier at the fruit stand knew I was befuddled much of the time, so she always very slowly counted back the change to me. Once I went into a shop to look for a dress. After some awkward exchange, half-French, half-English, the clerk asked in English if I was shopping for myself to which I replied, "*Oui.*" She shot a strange look over to the other clerk, and some subtle but very polite snickering ensued. Simultaneously, I caught sight of a mannequin with an over-sized tummy, and realized that I was in a maternity shop! There was nothing left to do but laugh at myself which gave them permission to laugh with me. We said a polite *au revoir* (good-bye), and I hightailed it back onto the street. It was not the last time I would be embarrassed in Paris.

We were steps away from the *Saint-Paul Métro* stop, the *lavomatique* (coin-operated laundromat), a couple of fresh fruit markets, a cheese shop, a florist, a dry cleaner, privately owned bookstores (which have sadly closed), and plenty of ladies' dress and shoe shops. Probably within a mile of our apartment were at least a hundred different street cafés and restaurants, and I'm not exaggerating. We discovered three grocery stores, including a *Monoprix*, a couple of hairdressers, a barber shop for Bernie, a post office nearby, and even a branch of the *SNCF*, the French train system, where we could easily purchase train tickets to anywhere in Europe.

It's important to say a word more about the *Saint-Paul Métro* station. Because it doesn't connect to other subway lines, it's easy to navigate and never very busy. It even has an ascending escalator at the exit. It is part of Line 1 which was the first subway line built to serve the center of Paris flowing east/west. A busy hub where multiple lines intersect can be a pain in the *derrière* (rear), so we find *Saint-Paul* just to our liking. In front of the subway entrance is a taxi stand, which makes getting to the airport a breeze on the return trip.

Every year, Bernie is on the look-out for our familiar homeless guy, who occupies the stairway going down into the station. Last year, he wasn't there at first, and we both had a sense of sadness that perhaps he had passed. Then all of a sudden, he appeared one day. Bernie sang out, "Ah, look, there's our guy. Wonder where's he's been?"

No way to know the answer, but seeing him certainly made us feel at home.

RIDING LE MÉTRO HAND-IN-HAND

Your first big act of couple courage inside the city of Paris will be stepping into a subway station. I was lucky my first time because I had Bernie, "the *Métro* pro." *Le Métropolitain* looks and smells old because it's been around for a hundred and fifty years. Most stations are constantly being upgraded with new lighting, and many are now automated with no drivers. If you've never ridden subway systems at all, study up on them because they all function essentially the same way. There are a few basic tricks to *Le Métro*:

* Buy a *carnet* of ten tickets in the station; or if your stay is more than a week, check on other options with the station attendant—three, five, or seven-day passes. For our two-month stay, I use

something called a *Navigo* card which I load the first Monday of each month. It's easy and ticketless. Bernie is still using a ticket that is seven or eight years old because someone forget to enter an end date when it was purchased. Yes, it has been our Golden Ticket! (Alas, summer of 2016, the ticket finally stopped working. Bernie plans to frame it.)

* Keep your ticket handy until you exit the station in case the "subway police" stop you and demand to see it. Once outside, tear it up and toss it in the green garbage cans. If you don't, I guarantee that you will mix it up with the valid tickets and try to use it again.

* Know your final destination to determine which signs to follow.

* Be prepared to see and sit next to all kinds of people.

* Sit quietly with little chatter. Parisians maintain their privacy in very close quarters like the subway with the exception of the teenage gals who babble away.

* Enter and exit the cars quickly as the doors close **with a vengeance**. Don't try to beat the doors by running on at the last minute. You'll be sorry!

* Observe how to open and close the doors. Some are automatic; others require pushing a button; others, flipping a handle.

* There is often standing room only. And on your first ride, you will likely lose your balance as the subway is zipping off, landing you in a stranger's lap. Laugh together, and grab the center pole! It happens all the time, and Parisians are used to it.

* Changing from one line to another is referred to as *la correspondance* and requires using a subway map that you keep on your person or find on the walls of each station. Look for the number of the new intersecting line you need and just follow the signs. You'll mess up a few times, but that's part of the fun.

* Have a plan in case you get separated! The best idea for newcomers is for the one ahead to wait at the next station.

One of the very attractive *Métro* stations

Approach the subway like a new adventure, and don't let it intimidate you. Explore it, ask for help, and realize that taxis are both expensive and sparse! Walking is the only way to see Paris as a couple, and the subway is a necessity to that end. Support and encourage each other; be forgiving when you screw up; laugh a lot; enjoy the music; endure the beggars, and be grateful for deodorant!

I should probably mention that the city buses are a viable alternative if you just can't seem to get your courage up for *Le Métro*. The outside scenery is certainly better and far fewer steps. However, to me the bus maps and route times are harder to read; the wait times are frustrating if you don't know the routes well; the trips take longer because of frequent stops, and seating can be sparse. It's often a stroller brigade of young mothers who prefer this mode of transportation to all the steps into and out of *Le Métro*. Older folks also prefer the bus. Did I just say that?

As you enter, ride, and leave *Le Métro*, beware of pickpockets. Bernie was almost robbed once just as he was about to get off an escalator. He felt something funny, turned, and saw a guy's hand in his pocket. He screamed profanity at him in familiar French, almost took the guy's head off with a karate chop, and that was the end of that! The pickpocket couldn't run fast enough. Guys, put your wallets in your front pocket; ladies, sling your purse over your neck and across your shoulder, hugging it into your chest. Be assertive, careful, and aware *all the time*.

Purely Paris

Enjoy the varied subway entertainment and give a coin only if you feel so inclined. We've seen everything from magicians to puppet shows on the subways and in the stations—a wonderful part of the personality of Paris.

Le Temps (The Weather)

I believe it rained more the sixty days we were in our first apartment than at any of our other visits to Paris. Usually, rainstorms blow up quickly and last just an hour or two. But that summer of 2007, the rain came early and stayed all through the day, pouring down in bucket loads. Many days were long and dreary, and the summer was plain cold. On one of our side trips to visit Bernie's cousins in the southeastern part of France, it was so cold I had to buy closed-toed shoes. Jean-Paul, Bernie's cousin, told us that it was one of the coldest Julys on record. I never went anywhere without my umbrella. A long raincoat, which I thought would be an unnecessary extra, became my daily companion. I read volumes and watched hours of British television, save for the twenty-four-hour French news channel, *France Vingt-Quatre* (France 24). Smile—it is a French channel but televised both in English and French; we, of course, watched the English version. Remember—it's complicated.

Weather can be your biggest enigma in Paris—plan for everything and expect nothing. Forget about checking into normal temps prior to your arrival. You will have less frustration that way. Dress for the day and always have an umbrella, a scarf and a pair of socks. Paris is on the same latitude as Bangor, Maine, Nova Scotia, and Newfoundland. You can have a winter-like day in summer and a summer-like day in early spring or fall. The street clothes that Parisians wear follow suit, regardless of the season. If it's a cold July day, men will don wool sports coats, and women will layer up in black.

Les Gens (The People)

The French phrase for people in general is *les gens*. Wow, did I have a lot to learn about them! I knew one French person, Bernie, who was a thoroughly Americanized version. If you heard him speak English today, you would detect nothing of a French accent; remember, he has been in America since he was ten years old. The French crush him when they say that he speaks French with an American accent. Ouch!

I didn't realize how very important it was to greet every clerk, every waiter, and every grocery checker with a *Bonjour, madame or monsieur*. I didn't know to always say *au revoir* or *bonne journée* (have a good day) when leaving a store, or that it was rude to leave food on your plate. I didn't know that I shouldn't eat my French fries or my sandwich with my fingers—that is changing. Thank goodness I had read up on the importance of being ultra-polite. I discovered that I could communicate with the waiters using my eyes and gestures *sans* (without) a word of French. I learned quickly the very demonstrative sayings like *oh là là* which say volumes without words. I learned to keep my distance, as the French are not Southerners who will talk to anybody about anything. I quickly observed not to talk loudly on the subway. However, Parisians will join in on your political conversations at sidewalk cafés. When Hillary and Obama were competing for the Democratic nomination, people were all ears.

The French practice the Golden Rule—be nice to them and they will be nice to you. It's quite simple. The French are also patient people. They tolerate and give money to the beggars and street performers; they feed the pigeons; they help strangers carry baby strollers and luggage up the long subway steps; they're always eager to give you directions. They wait patiently in long lines; ride shoulder to shoulder in hot, crowded subways; wait for thirty to forty-five minutes just to get a cone of *Berthillon* ice cream; and never demand quick service from a waiter. They lead a less stressful life and always enjoy a long lunch with lots of red wine. How interesting that when I have scanned my credit card at the grocery store, the display reveals the word *Patience* (Wait) while the entry is processing.

LA BAGUETTE (THE BREAD)

The long stick of French bread called *une baguette* is the classic symbol of French daily life and the Holy Grail to people like Bernie. *Pain* (silent n) is the French word for bread, and it's one of the first words repeated by young tots. There are significant differences, according to Bernie, in these slender, unsliced slabs of bread. He can discriminate; I cannot. Whereas you and I might purchase one loaf of bread a week, Parisians may purchase two to four *baguettes* a day, depending on the size of their families. They are rarely ever wrapped, except for a small pastry paper folded around the center. Rarely have I seen Parisians butter their bread, except sometimes when eating cheese, and never have I been served a small saucer of olive oil and herbs with the bread as you might have in Italy or America. They eat the bread mostly before their meal and break it into small pieces. The price of the generic *baguette* is set by the government and is about a *euro* or just over a dollar in American money. Being a baker of bread is an esteemed vocation. Dressed all in white, bakers work through the night and wee hours of the morning to have enough bread to feed the masses. There is much hoopla annually over who claims the status as best bread-baker, and to be named in the top five is a coveted and much publicized honor!

The streets are abuzz in the early evening as people get off work and stop at the local *boulangerie* to purchase bread for the evening meal. In our immediate area, our favorite *boulangerie,* and one of the busiest, is *Miss Manon.* Bernie makes the daily run first thing in the morning when the bread is still warm and freshly baked and then again in the afternoon. Going to the *boulangerie* is exciting to him! He is now recognized at *Miss Manon* as a frequent customer, which adds to the fun.

Purely Paris

Stand in line at a popular *boulangerie* and inhale the smell of freshly baked bread. Grab a baguette and eat it together as you're walking down the street for an afternoon snack.

<u>A Best Bet while in Paris:</u> Hotel Caron
This quaint hotel in the heart of the *Marais* district is a jewel and has hosted several of our friends. It is a block off *rue Saint-Antoine,* nestled next to the very lovely *Sainte-Catherine Square.* The staff are extremely helpful; the hotel is air-conditioned, has a free mini-bar, offers extremely good security and a breakfast for only 14 euros (cheap for Paris). It also has free internet, Wi-Fi connections, and a free *Herald Tribune* in the mornings. It has a great web site at *www.hotelcaron.com.* If an apartment is not for you, and you want to stay in the *Marais* without breaking the bank, this is our recommendation.

Les Cafés et un café (The Cafés and a Coffee)
The French have the same word for their sidewalk eateries (old coffee houses) as they have for coffee which is certainly appropriate since both are such a part of daily life.

Paris would not be Paris without the sidewalk cafés. Picture this—tiny tables for two often imprinted on top with artwork and pushed together tightly in rows that only the waiter controls. The bases are ornamental, albeit heavy ironwork, and most of the chairs are caned in familiar French design with small colored strands woven into the pattern. (Check out the web site on *Maison Drucker* café chairs: *http://www.walterswicker.com/collections/drucker-french-bistro.html*.) Heaters usually grace the exterior on long poles, and colored awnings are rolled in and out to protect customers from sun and rain. The cafés are literally everywhere, and just like *boulangeries*, everyone has a favorite. Parisians love to gather and talk, debate, laugh, and imbibe. I would lay bets that your fondest dose of cultural immersion will be the sidewalk café. Generally, these have little to do with the food and more to do with proximity to your apartment, people-watching, and the camaraderie or *la joie de vivre* (the love of life) shared with friends and waiters. For the price of a cup of coffee or a glass of wine, you can rent a table for the entire afternoon. No one pressures you to finish or makes you feel guilty for taking up the space. You can read, sunbathe, nap, or chat with friends for as long as you wish. It's truly wonderful. Of if you're Bernie, you can sit and take pictures. He's perfected the process of hiding his very sophisticated camera below table level to catch the sights and sounds of traffic, relationships, animals, arguments, passionate lovers, and playful waiters. Remember in Paris, one must be discreet! It was not until two years ago that we learned it was illegal to take pictures of small children!

And yes, a kind word for the waiters at sidewalk cafés. Most are dressed in the typical white shirt, black vest and bowtie, and starched white apron over black trousers. They work very hard, luring in and serving hundreds of customers every day, somehow squeezing between the tables in rapid efficiency. In many cases, their patrons just want an *espresso*, a glass of wine, a beer, or a Coca-Light. These guys and a few gals are fast, mostly polite, and full of clever antics. Occasionally, you run into a sour puss but not often. They like to recognize you and give better service if you're a frequent patron. There is an issue of turnover, and we're always disappointed to find that a favorite waiter from the previous year has moved on. We assume that waiters in the better restaurants make good money. Being a waiter in a starred restaurant is a highly rated profession. They train for many months to win a coveted position, and one mistake can find them out of a job.

Let's talk about the beverage now, *café* (coffee). It is offered not only at the sidewalk cafés but also at every bistro, brasserie, and restaurant. *Un café* (a coffee) comes in many shapes and sizes. An *espresso* is generally about the same wherever you go: strong and small and the most popular. And some places serve a little *gateau* (sweet cookie or cake) or *chocolat* with the café. Those are my favorites! *Café au lait* or *café crème* (coffee with milk) is generally a morning drink with breakfast; *cappuccinos* are most always on the menu but more expensive; *café americain* (American coffee) has been watered down and is served in a larger cup. The waiters will patiently serve it to you, but I've learned to order it less frequently. One could never become a real Parisian without loving the strong coffee. Depending on what you order and where you are when you order it, *un café* will run somewhere between €2.60 and €4.20 ($3-$6). In recent years, Starbuck's locations have been popping up profusely. The Parisians flock to them, and we don't know exactly why—perhaps more coffee for their money as suggested by Bernie or just the obsession with anything American. We generally refuse to go in one as it seems almost a betrayal to us.

OTHER CULTURAL TIDBITS TO ENHANCE YOUR DAILY LIVING EXPERIENCE

Time is different in Paris. The city gets moving around ten o'clock. Lunch is served any time between noon and four o'clock; dinner, between eight and ten o'clock. Stores often close two hours for lunch; the fruit stands often close between one-thirty and three-thirty in the afternoons, and many shops don't open at all on Mondays. Adherence to a posted time schedule is not a big French priority. Getting upset about that as a visitor only diminishes your experience; it doesn't bother the Parisians. Our best advice is to set your body clock to the rhythm of the French day—go to bed around midnight and get up at eight.

It's worth repeating that politeness is the magic answer to receiving great treatment in Paris. Being forceful, demanding, or impatient (as many Americans can be) creates a stubbornness that will spoil your visit. Don't try to make Paris like America. I've watched episode after episode of rude Americans trying to scream their way into better, faster service at hotels and cafés with no success. One of the more memorable happened at the very popular *Café de Flore* on the Left Bank. There was a long line to be seated, and an American couple grew outwardly impatient with the *maître d'hotel* (head waiter), loudly and impolitely telling him how long they had been waiting. The Frenchman tried patiently to explain and apologize. When the couple finally were seated, it took a while for them to be acknowledged by their regular waiter, which is customary. Eventually, they huffed out with unpleasant language, all overheard by me. I wanted to spank both of them. The French rarely show their anger, but you can certainly sense their disgust, as was the case on that day. Ugly Americans should stay home!

Lunches are two hours; dinners are three because eating is a Parisian pleasure to be fully enjoyed. Many companies give an extended lunch hour to their employees. Three tips: Put your menu face down when you are ready to order; cross your knife and fork across the breadth of your plate when you're finished; and you will most likely not receive your check unless you ask for it, "*L'addition, s'il vous plaît*." Even then, it may be another thirty minutes before you finish the process. This one still bugs me, but I'm getting better! The one exception to this elongated exercise is in some of the high-tourist street cafés where the waiter may present your tab with your order and expect immediate payment.

A technical advance used at most eating places is *La Machine*. It resembles a large, hand-held calculator which scans your card, approves it, and prints the receipt in your presence. Your card is never out of your sight. We can't understand why we don't have more of these in America. Perhaps it's because we don't have a fixed percentage automatically added for the tip as the French do—18%. It would be a profitable business opportunity for someone who could figure it out.

As to cleanliness, the element of personal hygiene is not an issue anymore in Paris. The old stereotypical jeers about the French who didn't bathe or use deodorant are a thing of the past. The Parisians do not, however, share our obsession with germs and bacteria. It's not that they are dirty; it's more an acceptance that Paris is a dusty, old city where space is tight, people are relaxed, and cleanliness is relative. They try very hard against great odds. I have struggled with our apartment, trying diligently at first to keep it clean, but slowly realizing that clean is different here. Also, you constantly see people walking down the street with unwrapped baguettes under their arms, and dogs being allowed in the restaurants with eagerness. Let's just say that our health departments would go crazy.

The street cleaners are amazing. They perform their magic all day, sweeping and washing the streets and the subways. If you are seated at a sidewalk café when they begin this clean-up, you may get sprayed—not my favorite part of Parisian life! Doggie poop used to be rare with the requirement to use pooper-scoopers; however, in the past several years, we've dodged more and more surprises on the sidewalks. There are bright green litter cans with green plastic bags on every corner. The Green Team, as Bernie calls them, changes the bags all day long, and the garbage trucks run from early morning to midnight. Am I suggesting that there is no litter on the streets of Paris? No—but I am applauding the great effort made to keep Paris a clean, lovely city. Trips to other *arrondissements* have shown us that not all areas of Paris are as well-kept as our beloved *Marais*.

Paris does an incredible job with recycling. Waiters at the cafés carry huge crates of wine bottles from their eating establishments to gigantic green recycling barrels along the main streets. Many a morning, Bernie and I sit straight up in bed when these are emptied right outside our windows! The crashing glass is deafening. Our apartment building has huge bins in the downstairs courtyard for glass, newspaper, and plastic, and we dutifully separate and recycle everything.

According to Bernie's family, religion is a dying force in France. As was stated to us, "People are baptized Catholic, married Catholic, and buried Catholic; but in between, there's not much activity." In the churches we visit, however, we see signs of active parish life, with both young and old. If attending church is important to you and you want a service in English, try the American Cathedral of Paris located on *Avenue Georges V,* which is off *Les Champs Elysées.* It is high Anglican, so it will suit both Catholics and Protestants. The sanctuary is impressive with flags and needlepointed prayer benches for each of the fifty American states. We go at least once each visit and always find it meaningful. Afterward, try lunch at *La Fermette Marbeuf* or the garden room at the *Georges V Hôtel.* More on these later.

The mayor of Paris makes thousands of rental bikes available to the residents and tourists to encourage less traffic, more exercise, and a spirit of independent fun—all easily engaged by one swipe of your credit card. Cell phones, iPods, BlackBerries, all the latest technology are **everywhere**, and people are just as rude here talking loudly on their cell phones as they are in America. This was a surprising disappointment to Bernie. Mostly, it's the young people who walk, shop, ride the subway, go to the bathroom, and run into you—while talking. Laptop computers are also everywhere, and many folks work on their computers as they ride the subway. Yes, Parisians can get both cell service and internet connectivity inside the subway!

Cigarette smoke is everywhere, much to my dismay; and cigarette butts make up a significant piece of the litter challenge. The prevalent iron grates at the base of large trees in public areas are magnets for the cigarette butts—very unsightly despite a recent effort to clean them out. The push to stop smoking has definitely hit Paris over the course of our eleven years of visiting. Initially, all the eating places both inside and out were full of smokers, which drove me nuts. Now all restaurants are non-smoking, even in the bars; however, that has pushed smokers to the outside tables where we like to sit! It's the young people who seem to smoke most prevalently, especially the females. On French packs of cigarettes, instead of reading as ours do that cigarette smoking can be hazardous to your health, their packs say, "Cigarettes Kill."

What about restrooms? The dependable spot for a clean restroom without making a purchase is a McDonald's or a Starbuck's. Fortunately, or unfortunately, they are around every corner. It is a definite no-no to enter a French restaurant to use the toilette unless you are a patron. Don't shy away from the street toilets; most are new, clean, and affordable in an emergency. They cost one euro and are washed down completely after each use. Initially, I turned up my nose, but now I don't hesitate! Ladies, keep a small pee-pee purse inside your big purse containing some Kleenex (just in case) and small coins. If you have to pay at a toilet in parks or in the occasional restaurant, it's only forty or fifty cents. If the lights suddenly go out in the restroom stall, don't panic. It will be pitch-black scary; just wave your arms above your head, and the motion-sensitive lights will come back on. To find the restroom in a café or restaurant, look for the steps up or down! Memorize the phrase, *"Où sont les toilettes?"* (Where are the restrooms?)

At the fabulous street markets, don't touch the fruit! That means you can't hand pick the cherries. The vendors will reprimand you sharply! Go to the same market repeatedly, and you will find friendlier service; however, you still can't touch the fruit! But you can select your own cherries at the *Monoprix!*

Buy your wine from the grocery store, not an independent seller, unless, of course, you're a true connoisseur, want exclusive brands, and eager to pay extravagant prices. The selections are plentiful, especially at the *cave* in the *Monoprix* on *rue Saint-Antoine* in the *Marais,* and the prices are unbelievably low. Bernie's favorite, *Côtes du Rhône,* is about five dollars.

If you're game for some daily living in Paris, come with lots of money and patience, and a body that's in good shape. Prepare to walk **at least** three miles a day, plus up and down dozens of steps. Many areas are cobblestone, which makes walking doubly difficult. Finally, lose five to ten pounds before coming so you can enjoy the desserts. The walking will take care of some of the calories, but not all!

Daily living might be a struggle for you initially, but for us, it's pure paradise! Bernie and I cruise into slow, easy mornings, enjoying many cups of strong coffee, checking finances online, working a crossword puzzle, and maybe watching a little CNN to stay on top of the home front. We may not leave out for our day's jaunt until eleven o'clock, and more often than not, that's a trip to the grocery store. We haggle over whether to eat lunch in the apartment or go out, and much of our decision-making depends on the weather. Later in the book, we'll share some fun outings for both sunny days and rainy days.

Purely Paris:

The best dessert at *Le Bouquet Saint-Paul* is *mousse au chocolat* served in a glass mason jar with a locked wire lid! Absolutely yummy for a first night in Paris. Check it out if you're in *Le Marais.*

Endure the begging. It happens here as in all big cities. "*Non, merci*" is the polite response except with the gypsies who can be rude and overbearing. You may have to be rude back and insist that they leave you alone. Be careful because as they are engaging you in conversation, they could be trying to slip your wallet out of your pocket or purse!

Go on picnics at least once a week if you want to be truly Parisian. The *Franglais*, half French-half English, is *pique-nique*. The menu is easy and cheap—ham sandwich, fruit, cheese, wine and *chocolat*! Find your favorite green space in a neighborhood park or in the grand parks like *Les Tuileries, Le Jardin du Luxembourg* or *Parc Monceau.* Or just go down to the river and find a bench! Go in the evening along the river, and watch how the Parisians do it. They spread out big blankets and invite all of their friends to bring a covered dish. Great people-watching!

CHAPTER 6

Arguing in Paris

Disputes à Paris

~ে~

I like Frenchmen very much, because even when
they insult you, they do it so nicely.

– JOSEPHINE BAKER

YOU SHOULD KNOW THAT, IN the States, Bernie and I don't live together, and we don't see each other until late in the day. We have dinner every evening and then enjoy each other's company until around ten o'clock. Long ago, we made the decision not to marry. Having failed in two marriages already, I didn't want to try for a third. Like many couples our age, we decided to pay attention to red flags instead of blowing past them. The wisdom of age is knowing that we're not going to change the other one! We wanted peace, friendship, reliable companionship, someone to trust, someone to grow old with, and someone who made us feel safe and loved. That's a tall order, but we would both avow success!

In Paris, everything slips into a slightly different gear composed of seven parts romantically wonderful and one-part petty reality. We live under the same roof for two months, spending almost every waking moment side by side and scrutinizing each other's every move. It should come as no surprise that this breeds tension, the need for touchy negotiation on daily decisions, and ultimately some spats. We share this chapter in the spirit of telling a **real** story and to humorously answer the question, "What can a couple argue about in the City of Light and Love?" Well, the simple answer for us, thank goodness, is—not much of any significance. We hope our honesty will produce a chuckle or two, and prevent a meltdown with your lover while you're in Paris!

The biggest challenge for us is the speed at which we live out our days, driven by our different personalities. As I referenced earlier, I am always cranked, impulsive, and running in fast speed; Bernie is generally idling in first gear with a pleasant reflectiveness. We are truly the tortoise and the hare. At home, this doesn't bite us because of how we structure our day. But in Paris, the cohabitation compounds everything. For example—how fast we get ready for the day, how we plan for daily outings, how we process details, whether it be for a dinner reservation or train tickets to Lyon or the itinerary for company. I'm always pushing for action, and Bernie is content to glide along. I'm insisting on handling it **now**, and he's resisting with "what's the hurry?" It's what I call the "push-pull" of Paris, and we can almost drive each other crazy—almost. When I've reached my max point, my solution is to go shopping or take a walk. His is to take a nap. Tortoise and the hare!

Another rub is traffic safety in Paris. The traffic lights are very clear as to when it's time to cross a street. You either get a red man or a green man symbol. Bernie, like most Parisians, pays little attention to the lights; he walks when he's ready, which sometimes leaves me dangling on the street corner! Then he gets quite upset because I didn't break the law, risk the traffic, and follow after him. He stands on the opposite side of the street and glares at me! Once I was so angry that I refused to walk on the same side of the street with him! So, yes, we have had our worst disagreements over this little tidbit of idiocy—even gone a day without speaking! One day, Bernie didn't look, stepped off the curb, and suddenly we heard the screech of bus tires and the horn of a furious bus driver. The bus stopped within inches of Bernie's body. Ultimately, I have made the decision to cross the street when I feel safe **regardless** of what Bernie does. Over time, I've become almost as bad as he is and walk against the light if the coast is clear. Yes—I'm becoming a true Parisian! You can imagine that I never hear the end of this—but all in fun.

Another frustration between us can fire up over the umbrella. I **never** head out in Paris without an umbrella as rain storms pop up like sprouting weeds. Bernie thinks this is absurd. He's oblivious to hair, to clothes, to dirty puddles; he walks in pouring rain and vows that it's hardly raining. It's a twenty-two-year military conditioning as best I can figure. He has spent days and nights in the rain and mud, without a thought. I will not win this one. I have a light-weight umbrella that fits in what I call my "by-God" Paris purse, and I take it with me every day. I don't even offer anymore to share it with him, regardless of how hard it is raining. He considers it an affront to his Army toughness!

The call for extreme politeness with the French has occasionally created tension for us. For example, after waiting a generous thirty minutes after finishing a meal, I will turn to Bernie and say, "Have you asked for the check?"

Remember, this is easily accomplished by the gesture of pretending to write in the palm of your hand while saying, "*L'addition, s'il vous plaît.*" (the check, if you please.)

"No, not yet. I haven't finished my wine, and we're not in any hurry, are we?" he will say with an unhappy face.

He is all too content to sit **indefinitely**, enjoying the ambiance, without getting rude or pushy.

"I'm going to the ladies' room," I announce standing, hoping this will be his cue. But upon returning, I see that no progress has been made.

"Have you not asked for the check yet, Bernie?" I say with disgust in my tone.

"I'm trying to, but I haven't been able to get the waiter's attention," Bernie will snap defensively.

Ugh, how long does it take? I've gotten better about ignoring this irritation both from him and the waiters, but once in a while, I explode.

It has taken me a while to accept that our relationship purrs along better if I realize who's ultimately in charge. It **is** Bernie's Paris, after all, and I'm smart to remember that. I recall with still a knot in my stomach, the first time his son visited. We had moved to a different apartment to give them ours on *rue Saint-Paul*. We excitedly walked up the thirty-four steps to present the first view of their living space. I was politely trying to explain a few things about the kitchen when Bernie just about snapped my head off, letting me know in clear, definitive, profane aggravation that it was his place to take the lead on sharing information. After he barked so loudly at me, I stormed out, making an awkward scene worse for everyone. Furious and embarrassed, I never forgot that he is and always will be **the** French authority and the alpha dog! There was never an apology!

Does this all sound familiar? It's like who squeezes which end of the tube of toothpaste or how often the toilet seat is left up. The major issues, thank goodness, don't seem to bother us in Paris, but, just like all couples, the grinding, gnawing, minuscule particulars can sometimes wear us thin. I must say that we let them go quickly and without harboring a grudge; we rarely go to bed angry. Every day is a new day, and we let the memory of yesterday's blips slip by like birthdays. The good so outweighs the bad that it's easy to maintain a steady perspective. We never allow the disagreements to get out of hand or ruin our trip. Bernie gets more credit here than I do because he's the most forgiving person I have ever known, and it's impossible to harbor anger towards him for very long.

If you're planning a trip to Paris with your spouse or lover, get ready for some tension as you go through the day. If your relationship is testy anyway or if your personalities run on opposite cylinders, you might want to go with a tour group, where all the daily decisions are made for you. But if you've got courage and want to do it the authentic way, grab each other's hands and figure out cute ways to resolve your differences when they arise. Laughter helps. Embrace those two-hour lunches and three-hour dinners along with the wine which flows like a tumbling waterfall. In the grand scheme of life, the irritations are nothing to compare with getting to spend time together in a city made for lovers.

Purely Paris

Sometimes when crossing a wide, multi-lane boulevard, there may be two sets of lights—one on the side of the street and one out in the middle, and they are not necessarily in sync. Pay close attention! On the traffic light posts, you can push walk buttons to make the light change. Never step off the curb on a busy boulevard without a green man. The buses will roll over your toes!

CHAPTER 7

Oh, My Goodness!

Oh là là!

∽

Boy, those French, they have a different word for everything.

— STEVE MARTIN

IF YOU RENT AN APARTMENT for a while and immerse yourselves in Parisian daily life, you'll notice that bizarre scenarios happen around you frequently. Bernie and I embrace these as part of the wide-open charm of Paris. They are often paired with the contagious, colloquial expression, *Oh là là*—uttered in disbelief or comical frustration. We dub it as the ultimate French expression. It's kin to our "Holy smokes," "Oh, my gosh," or "Good grief!" Even the elite say it under their breaths. Americans can't quite replicate the phrase exactly as the French say it. They roll it off curled tongues from somewhere deep in their throats. And if they get really agitated, the phrase can stretch out to *Oh là là là là là là* joined by a roll of their eyes, a smirky grin, and hands thrown up in the air.

Paris has given us many *Oh là là!* moments where we look at each other and say, "This can't be happening!" Here are some of our best.

LINDA ALMOST ROBBED

Several years ago, we were meandering in and out of shops around *La Place de la Madeleine*, with mobs of other people. Bernie had ducked into a store to purchase a bottle of water for me. That particular day I was carrying a small, top-zippered purse with a shoulder strap. It was a recent gift and not my usual pocketbook. All of a sudden, amid the pushing and pulling of the crowd, I felt something odd. I looked down, and there was a hand in my purse pulling out all of my €20 bills! I grabbed the hand, that of a teenage girl, and screamed, "What are you doing?"

She dropped the bills and ran. I'm not sure what came over me; but I ran after her, grabbed her from the back by the shoulders, whirled her around, and screamed at her some more, telling her not to ever bother me again. I was furious and undoubtedly stupid for confronting her. Almost immediately, a plain-clothes police woman appeared at my side.

"Did she get any money?" she asked breathlessly as she pulled out her badge and shoved it in my face.

My head was spinning, trying to make sense of the attempted robbery and then the sudden appearance of the police woman at my side.

"No!" I answered proudly, "I grabbed her hand and screamed at her, then chased her down."

The policewoman seemed disappointed and said sternly, "She is part of a teenage gang that we've been chasing all day. I was hoping she had gotten something out of your purse; then I could have arrested her."

The cop was miffed at **me** because I had thwarted the robbery and then took off after the gang of girls. I was left scratching my head. Bernie missed the entire drama, but my friend Jeanie Thompson was witness to it all. *Oh là là!*

CONCERT AT SAINTE-CHAPELLE

Sainte-Chapelle is a Paris treasure, located on *Ile de la Cité* on the grounds of the Department of Justice. Dating back to the thirteenth century, this chapel was commissioned by Louis IX and contains one of the most extensive and exquisite collections of stained glass anywhere in the world. With near perfect acoustics, the chapel hosts regular concerts almost every week. Held in the late afternoon, the concerts play host to the sun's piercing rays as they filter through the stained glass windows, producing a kaleidoscope of brilliant color—truly magnificent.

Beautiful stained glass at *Sainte-Chapelle*

The *oh là là* moment for us happened at a Vivaldi concert in 2007. The French, not surprisingly, are very proper at their concerts. During a break between movements, an elderly woman's cell phone started playing its own tune. The acoustics in the chapel amplified the volume and drew attention to the unexpected interruption! With all eyes upon her, she was frantically pushing buttons, trying to turn off her phone. But the harder she tried to stop it, the worse it became. The performing group and the conductor, with arms up and poised, waited patiently for the phone to quit. Just when everyone thought it was under control, the musicians would begin to play, and the phone would start again. This happened three or four times. The crowd grew impatient, not to mention the performers, and finally, the gentleman seated beside the poor lady grabbed her phone brusquely out of her hand and turned it off. She was humiliated; concert goers were miffed, but Bernie and I wanted to laugh out loud. The French formality was no match for modern-day technology. I'm quite sure that someone in that concert hall was muttering *Oh là là* under his breath!

BAMA GIRLS UPSTAIRS

You recall that our neighbors upstairs have taken a portion of their large, top-floor flat and turned it into a two-person suite to lease. Several years ago, they told us that two girls from the University of Alabama would be arriving soon to rent out the space. We thought, "What a small world!" Later that week as we were going up the thirty-four steps to our apartment, we wondered whether the Alabama gals had arrived yet. Without warning, Bernie leaned out over the railing by our front door and yelled up, "Roll Tide!" which in case you don't know is the battle cry for the Crimson Tide of Alabama—surely everyone knows that. Instantly, two pretty heads popped out of the apartment window just like a double-sided jack-in-the-box. They were delighted to hear a familiar phrase, and we had a fun chat. I am quite sure it was the first time Bernard Verdier had ever uttered that phrase, and to know that it happened in Paris deserves an *Oh là là!*

FALLING FLOWER POT

This is a short story about the day I could have been killed in Paris. Walking down a narrow side street, I jumped at a crash right behind my back legs as something sprayed against them. I screamed and turned quickly to see the dirt and terra-cotta shards of a huge flower pot which had crashed down from two floors above us. People gathered around quickly asking if I was okay. And of course, I was— thanks to a few inches! We all looked up, and a tabby cat sat on the window ledge. He had jumped too aggressively and caused the large pot to topple out the window. It was funny, but yet it was not! If the heavy pot had landed on top of my head, well—you wouldn't be reading this book. *Oh là là!*

THE LAVOMATIQUE

The public laundry or *lavomatique* can be an amusing spot. I have met people from all over the world here, and we all share one thing in common—How the hell do we work these machines? The washing machines are like our new water-saving, front loaders, and the dryers are huge commercial sorts, large enough for multiple loads of laundry at one time. There is a separate wall display at the back for starting the machines, and you know this before I say it—it's complicated! There's also a way to buy a block of dry soap. The drying cycle is ten minutes per *euro*, and you can enter multiple cycles at one time. This is all easy to forget from one year to the next, and doubly tough for a first-time user!

Would you believe that one day, I met a guy from Tuscaloosa, Alabama, and we had a nice, long chat about Bama football as we're each folding our underwear! Another day, some ladies came in speaking Japanese. They were having a hard time with the directions and were obviously asking for my help. The language barrier was too great, and before I could say or do anything to stop them, they had dumped their block of soap powders into the dryer! *Oh là là!*

A DIP IN THE SEINE

On warm summer evenings, one of our enjoyable pastimes is to go for coffee after dinner and then walk along the river. One evening, our stroll was interrupted by sirens approaching from both land and sea—well, river. A wave of *gendarmes* (national police) and *les pompiers* (firemen) approached with lights and sirens, racing to a spot next to the river. At the same time, tearing around the island bend of *Ile Saint-Louis* came a police boat with flashing lights and sirens. As we stopped to pay closer attention, we immediately saw the problem. A young man had decided to take a dip in the *Seine*. There are plenty of "No Swimming" signs posted along the river, and the entry down is a good ten to fifteen feet, skidding along a heavily slanted, slick concrete bank. But this young man had decided it was his time to shine, and he had either jumped or slid into the water. We didn't see the beginning, just the aftermath. One thing was clear: this was no mistake or attempted suicide. He was splashing around and having a great time impressing his companions on the river bank, all of whom appeared slightly inebriated.

It was a prank he surely regretted when mounds of security descended upon him. And there we were at exactly the right place at the right moment to catch all the interesting commotion. Typical of the French, there was no great hoopla. They got him out of the water and then proceeded to have lengthy and calm conversation with him. We were on the opposite side of the river so could not hear any of the exchange. Finally, they did remove him from the site. Was he drunk too? Probably. But we will never know. It was a new twist on our summer *soirée—Oh là là!*

LES MANIFESTATIONS (DEMONSTRATIONS OR STRIKES)

Alas, the working class in France is always unhappy and dissatisfied with something or other— low wages, retirement benefits, working hours, working conditions, automation, you name it. The transportation workers are notorious for striking and taking the city hostage by withholding bus, train, or metro service, especially during peak tourist seasons.

In Paris, there is generally one location where their angst is revealed or "manifested" and that is at the large traffic circle known as *La Place de la Bastille.* It is named for the site of the old prison, and it's only two blocks from our apartment. Without warning in our third floor flat, we hear the piercing police whistles and then the rumble of multiple armed vehicles swishing past us on *rue Saint-Antoine.* Typically, I rush to the window and lean out as far as I can, stretching past the two-foot thickness of the sixteenth century wall to see what's happening, all the while screaming at Bernie, "Get the camera!"

What we witness is a convoy of twelve to fifteen riot-gear vehicles loaded with fully engaged *gendarmes* ready to take their stations at the Bastille. They look like gray aliens from outer space with gas-masks, bullet-proof vests, shields and assault rifles. They are followed by five or six buses (provided by the government) which hold the striking, disgruntled workers. The buses let everyone out, the strikers march around, some carrying signs, and others wielding megaphones. They shout and clap and march in passionate protest. The cops surround and patrol the area carefully in case there is any trouble; generally, the workers get back on the buses, and everything is fine.

Once was a little too close for comfort. I was out shopping by myself around the *Bastille*, looked up and saw the frenzy fast approaching. A second of confusion turned into some near panic as I quickly finished my business and rushed back to the apartment. I would never take the chance of getting caught in the middle of a manifestation because infrequently, as we've read in the news, things do not turn out well.

We live on one of the busiest thoroughfares in Paris, and I make frequent use of our window for catching these spectacles of Parisian culture. Bernie tires of grabbing his camera but I persist.

And there's no additional charge for this extracurricular activity!

IT'S COMPLICATED

I must admit that most things work pretty well in America, even though we love to bitch and moan to the contrary. Our systems are good, and most of the time when something goes awry, it can be easily fixed. Not so in Paris or France as a whole.

In June of 2011, we arrived in Paris about nine o'clock in the morning. We were just congratulating ourselves on the fact that no drama had beset us when Bernie suddenly realized that he had left his spiffy new phone with international coverage on the plane! Suddenly a pleasant welcome turned into a crazed frenzy as other travelers like us hovered around a tiny lost-and-found desk in the airport. Bernie was so upset with himself, but I reminded him of a lady (who shall remain nameless) who once left her wallet by a slot machine at the Bellagio Hotel in Vegas! As the bumper sticker says, "Stuff happens."

The officials contacted our airline, Open Skies, and they found the phone in Bernie's seat. We were so relieved. Just as someone was in route to return it to us, all the service handlers went on strike, and everything came to a screeching halt. Yes, we had indeed arrived in France, and yes, we immediately knew what tomorrow would bring.

We left our apartment the following day at one o'clock for what became a five-hour adventure, starting with two train tickets to *Orly* Airport for fifty dollars. Then we went from desk to desk, finally finding the airport official who had located Bernie's phone the day before. The phone had ended up in the main business office of Open Skies, which was out in a research park area called *Orly Tech*. After much confusion, we finally found the shuttle to take us out there. As we approached the building on foot, we noticed some people huddled around for a smoke break. We walked through them into a building with doors all around, marked *No access*. As we were standing there wondering where to go next, an attractive lady who had been smoking outside came bustling through the door calling, *"Monsieur Verdier?"* It was the lady who had the phone!! We almost hugged her. She was very kind and ran upstairs to retrieve it. Bernie immediately identified it as his, and we were off to retrace our steps. An hour later, we were back in the apartment, very happy with the day's progress and with surely four miles of walking under our belts.

As I have shared before, nothing is easy in Paris, even when one of us has command of the language. I shudder to think what this quest would have been like without Bernie's French.

MELODRAMA AT CHEZ PLUMEAU

One of the strangest dramas we've encountered in Paris happened in June of 2013 at *Chez Plumeau*, a favorite restaurant in *Montmartre*. We sadly discovered that the restaurant had been sold to new owners and was sporting a different menu. We were seated outside under the huge wisteria vines when suddenly a well-dressed lady with bright red hair started picking up the glasses from pre-set, unoccupied tables, smashing them onto the cobblestones—one—two—three—four! Glass was flying all around. She shattered four glasses, shouting something about how they belonged to her family. Then she started singing opera as she walked away into the crowd. Of course, all the wait staff darted after her. In typical French fashion, no one made a scene.

They spoke to her gently in hushed tones and eased her off the property and around the corner. Perhaps she was the previous owner or knew the previous owners. She came back another time and slipped inside, only to be escorted out. She had a very sad countenance, which was unnerving to me. The new owners made light of it, calling her crazy, but I couldn't help but wonder what the real story might be. Oh well, it was great fodder for our blog. And certainly another *Oh là là*!

Very frequently, friends and family from home ask us what we do every day in Paris. My answer is generally that "we just live." That response is met with question-mark grins, and a total lack of understanding. "Just living" here in Alabama is pretty hum-drum. In Paris, "just living" is wrapped in a polka-dot package peppered with unexpected twists that can happen on any jaunt, at any restaurant, during any stroll. It's the *Oh là là* magic of Paris. It's part of the allure, and why you must come!

Purely Paris

Expect little or no ice in eating establishments, generally only one or two tiny cubes. Parisians love Coke products and that has helped with availability. I still don't quite know what to do with the long spoon that is put in each slender glass—whether to drink with it in or out! Bernie doesn't either. If you find out, let us know!

CHAPTER 8

Only in Paris—Incredible

Seulement à Paris—Formidable!

He who contemplates the depths of Paris is seized with vertigo.
Nothing is more fantastic…Nothing is more sublime.

– Victor Hugo

LARGE CITIES LIKE PARIS HAVE a distinct personality, defined by landmarks, recurring events, parades, festivals, celebrations, and nicknames. This cultural DNA is why people love to visit. One of the best known for Paris is its famous moniker, "The City of Light" or *La Ville-Lumière,* a name it owes both to its fame as a center for education and ideas during the Age of Enlightenment and for its early adoption of street lighting. In more recent times, the wattage doesn't disappoint with dazzling lights all through the city.

How lucky we are to have tasted some of these "only in Paris" bits of culture. We can sing out *formidable or incroyable!* (fantastic, incredible) Here's our best to whet your appetite.

THE EIFFEL TOWER

La Tour Eiffel, as the French call it, is absolutely a touristy phenomenon, complete with mobs of visitors who move like waves under the massive iron legs.

Can it be a two-hour wait to go through the line at the bottom which only takes you up to the second tier? Absolutely. Can it be another two-hour wait to get to the very tip-top? Without question. Our plea—endure the waiting. Don't dare go to Paris without reserving a block of time to see the Eiffel Tower. Rising over a thousand feet, the imposing structure of delicate ironwork is itself daunting and magnificent, given that it was built in 1889. The cost to enjoy it is just fifteen to eighteen dollars per person depending on the euro-to-dollar ratio.

The Eiffel Tower

The first time you catch the view of Paris from atop the tower is jaw-dropping. That's why Bernie convinced me to wade through the hordes of people on our first trip. He knew that there was something majestic about the way the *Seine* twists and turns, about the lovely fountains graced by *Le Tracodéro* (huge plaza across from the Tower) in one direction, *L'Ecole Militaire* (military school) in the other, and *Les Champs de Mars* (massive green space) in between! He knew it was the best bird's-eye view, the signature vista of Paris.

Though controversial at first, even hated by the Parisians, it's now their defining tourist landmark. There are still a few locals who snobbishly dismiss the Tower as beneath their cultural standard; I don't agree, but then I'm a tourist! It lures people from around the globe as one of the most visited outside structures in the world. It exudes charm—the hustle and bustle of in-your-face street vendors, the aroma of messy food kiosks, the clatter of multiple foreign languages, and **always** the wedding photo shoots. We suggest that you go early in the morning or in the late afternoon to avoid some of the crowds. Or go as the darkness approaches and catch the top-of-the-hour light show when twenty thousand bulbs twinkle for five delicious minutes. For goodness sake, don't forget your camera. I've heard people say that they would never stand in the long lines. *Au contraire*! You can't miss it, even if it takes all day. You will forever cherish the memory; you just have to trust us on this one.

"Let's go back," Bernie said in 2015. "Let's walk the length of *Les Champs de Mars* about five o'clock and see if we can miss some of the lines! I also want to see the newly opened second tier and stand on the glass floor."

"Uh. . . I'm not so sure about the glass floor! I'll let you do that and I'll take your picture," I said, knowing that my motion sickness would likely kick in. "Let's go all the way to the top, one more time. Let's breathe in the majesty," I said with fondness.

"Then we'll have dinner at *The Wilson* across on the other side," Bernie suggested. "By the time dinner is over, we'll stand one more time and watch the twinkling lights."

"Sure, let's go! We need a few more pictures!"

THE PARIS AIR SHOW

Thanks to some very good connections in our hometown, we gained credentials to the world-famous Paris Air Show, which displays and demonstrates military and civilian aircraft to world-wide customers. In our high-tech, space city of Huntsville, Alabama, the Chamber of Commerce always sends a group to this event to scout out the latest and greatest in flying machines. We had tickets to the evening cocktail reception as well as general admission tickets for the show itself on the following day. So picture this. Here we are thousands of miles from home, going to a floating barge near the Eiffel Tower to join business executives from our hometown. It rained with a vengeance that night. The gorgeous view of the Tower was blocked by the wind and rains, but nothing dampened the hospitable time linking up with friends we knew.

The next morning, we headed out early for the show. The temperature was already in the high eighties with clear skies, signaling a hot day. The logistics were tough for first timers who had few connections. It took us an hour and a half to get in and an hour and a half to get out—not the same route. We probably walked five to six miles, given the subway/train ride. Just to print our E-passes at the entrance took forty-five minutes of waiting in line after we had walked thirty minutes from the train station to the show through the town of Bourget. Next was a forty-five-minute bus ride. Who knew it would be this complicated? Hmmm.

There were few signs, few bathrooms, few places to buy food, no place to sit down, and absolutely no shade. Duh, it's an airstrip. Of course, if we had been important, we would have had access to the *chalets* or hospitality suites where all of the amenities were flowing freely.

Bernie looked at me about noon and said, "Wow, it's really hot out here. Too bad we don't have credentials for the *chalets*!"

His almost bald head was in trouble.

The *halles* or exhibit areas were filled with sophisticated trade show booths, more intriguing to Bernie than to me, given his military background. The concourse outside where all the planes were on display was hot as blazes. We did watch some of the actual air show itself and saw the brand new Airbus take off and do its maneuvers, which enthralled the crowd and us. The plane was amazingly agile, given its size.

The most touching moment of the day came in mid-afternoon. Bernie's badge read "Retired Military." He so wanted to see inside a C-17, but the entry protocol was for invited guests only who were there on behalf of their company or their country. Bernie approached a young pilot who was with the Mississippi Air Guard, probably 24 or 25 years old. Pulling out his military ID card, Bernie said,

"I'd love to see inside that C-17, young man, but I don't have the right credentials. I served in Vietnam and used to jump out of C-130's."

"Sir!" the guardsman jumped to attention, saluted, and said, "Thank you for your service! Let me see what I can do."

He returned shortly and took us on a tour of the plane. Then he chatted with Bernie, anxious to hear his war stories and making no apology for his extreme dislike of Jane Fonda! He was just delightful and the highlight of our day. He said with a grin that he couldn't believe he'd gotten this fabulous assignment, much better than delivering supplies to Iraq or evacuating wounded soldiers. It was delightful to chat with a Southern boy from the States.

This hot day at the Paris Air Show remains a uniquely Parisian experience. It's not something we'd choose to do again. Once was enough, but once was great!

Le Tour de France

I never in my life had paid a whit of attention to *Le Tour de France*, an annual cycling event covering 2,100 miles in twenty-one days, always culminating in Paris. I may have known in the deepest recesses of my brain that it was a bicycle race, but that would be the gracious extent of my knowledge or interest. When I met Bernie, all of that changed. He gets so excited when he watches each day's race on television that his entire body quivers with enthusiasm. It is HIS sport. He's not a big college football fan, has absolutely no interest in baseball, will watch a little golf thanks to yours truly, and perhaps some pro football. But *Le Tour de France* commands his every brain wave.

Our first time to watch the grand finale of *Le Tour* on *l'Avenue des Champs Elysées* in 2008 was a day's worth of fun and excitement, eagerly anticipated. It was high on Bernie's bucket list. We had mapped out the subways that were going to be open and the streets that were set to be closed. Bernie had staked out the spot on *Les Champs* where he wanted to stand, and we went about six hours before the gaggle of racers was to arrive. One very important detail we failed to consider was a bathroom, which was a tough situation on this long day. Drink sparingly!

The sponsors' parade at *Le Tour de France*

We found ourselves in a mass of humanity from all over the world, gathered to watch the final spins along *Les Champs*. To the anticipated rhythm of the tap-tap-tap of bicycle wheels whizzing by on cobblestones, people were swarming with cameras, flags, stools, fierce loyalties, and beer. Did I say beer? Lots and lots of beer! The before-the-race parade, which began about four o'clock, was a surprise for us and well worth the time and energy to attend. Right before our eyes, the most sophisticated boulevard in Paris became a raucous, horn-tooting, rap-music-blaring brouhaha with clever floats, singing/dancing team members, and loud motorcycles. Eighteen-wheelers, which support each team, twisted and turned, honking their LOUD horns as they drove up *Les Champs*, circled around *l'Arc de Triomphe* and roared back down. The streets were packed with expectant fans, kiosks full of event merchandise, amd gigantic television screens—all adding to the Technicolor craziness.

We have attended *Le Tour* four times beginning with that first visit in 2008 when we stood for almost six hours. Contrast that with 2013's, last-minute visit. We arrived just in time to see a few passes of the *peleton,* the massive pack of bicyclists, and left in time to avoid the subway crush. It was *Le Tour's* 100th anniversary, and we couldn't stand to be in the apartment and miss a piece of history.

The final leg of *Le Tour de France* down *Les Champs Elysées*

We have seen Lance Armstrong three different times, twice when he won and once when he took second place. We were proud to wave our American flag as he whizzed by us. We are among those very disillusioned fans who revered Lance as an American hero and who now despise the fact that he turned out to be, of his own admission, a liar and a cheat.

For us, *Le Tour* will never be the same, *sans* Lance. But, it's still a must-see if you are lucky enough to be in Paris on the third Sunday in July. The event is free, usually but not always hot, and picture-friendly, if you can get a good viewing spot. Go early, take a stool, and be prepared to have last-minute fans walk up, absent any guilt at all, and break in front of you. Never mind that you've been standing for six hours. And remember, don't drink very much unless you have a cooperative bladder!

Over the years, the novelty has waned and with it, our fascination. I must admit that we are content now to watch *Le Tour* on television unless the entrance into Paris comes really close to our apartment. The one year it did, we had already departed! Bernie was crushed. I'm amazed at how much interest I have gained in *Le Tour*. It's a way to show my devotion to Bernie and affirm his love of the sport and the country which hosts it.

The annual finale of *Le Tour de France* – truly a Paris one and only!

Paris Plages

Since 2002, as a gift from the government, the mayor of Paris has provided a three-mile stretch of beach on the River *Seine* called *Paris Plages* (Paris Beach). What a spectacle! Tons of sand, palm trees, beach chairs, cabanas, trampolines, and volleyball nets are placed along the river to create the effect of being on the Riviera. Everything is donned in blue and white just like the actual beaches of Cannes. For one month, from about July 20 to August 20, all traffic is diverted from a major, river-side highway, allowing it to become a pedestrian walkway, the grand promenade for *Paris Plages*. Imagine how surprised we were the first time we saw the preparation.

"Is that sand over there?" asked Bernie with great curiosity, pointing across to the other side of the river.

"Well, it certainly looks like it, but why would they be putting sand next to the river?" I answered with confusion. We paid closer attention. I did a little research, and we followed day by day as the concept took shape. There was even a swimming pool the first couple of years, which has since disappeared, probably due to the expense. There are sidewalk cafés serving full meals, plenty of sophisticated porta potties with running water, water fountains, even a post office one year. How fun to see the Parisians in their bikinis and speedos! You can even surf—the internet that is. And always the Parisians dancing, singing, eating ice cream, rollerblading, and of course drinking a little wine. Fun, fun, fun!

We love an after-dinner stroll along the beach either alone or with company, and Bernie takes picture after picture as the daylight lingers until nine o'clock or so. We are rarely able to snag a beach chair, so we usually just stroll or walk over to the quad in front of *l'Hôtel de Ville* (the Paris City Hall) where sometimes there's a game of sand volley ball!

Parisians enjoying their beach, the *Paris Plages*

We have discovered that not everyone loves this venture. Some of our Parisian friends believe it is the height of socialism, using tax dollars to cater to the poor who cannot afford a vacation. We stay out of the politics and enjoy the ambiance, the wonderful people-watching, and the creative concept.

None of this costs a *centime*...the best things in life **are** free. We highly recommend that you try to plan your summer trip to coincide with *Paris Plages*—another Parisian signature extravaganza!

FÊTE DU PAIN

We're not always in Paris during the month of May, but 2008 was one of those years. One day, we happened upon *Le Fête du Pain* or The Celebration of Bread, an annual event held by the Mayor of Paris. Portable buildings had been erected in front of *Notre Dame,* which housed numerous display booths, and the aroma wafting from them was mouth-watering. The celebration was created in 1996 in honor of *Saint Honoré,* patron saint of bakers. (How delightful to be in a country where artisans still thrive. Reminiscent of the guilds of long ago, France still trains craftsmen in vocations like bread making that are passed down from generation to generation.) This festival hosts a competition of the best bread makers in and around Paris. Each year's winner has the honor of baking all the daily bread products for the President of France at the *Elysées* Palace for the entire next year. As we walked through the exposition, the bakers were handing out generous samples of various kinds of breads and cakes. The most popular group was from *Bretagne* which is next to *Normandy,* and they were dressed in native costumes with long flowing dresses and pointy white bonnets for the women. What a fun experience!

The artistry of bread baking

Bernie and I have often discussed how devastating it would be if Walmart entered France. It might destroy the lifeblood of the French economy: the mom-and-pop, family businesses, such as the *boulangeries*. Celebrations like the *Fête du Pain* help preserve this vital cultural distinction.

THE CATACOMBS

Lurking beneath the streets of Paris, south of the former city gate at today's *Place Denfert-Rochereau,* are the infamous catacombs. These caverns and tunnels are the remains of Paris' stone mines and have been open to the public since 1874. They were closed briefly in 2009 due to vandalism. Because of the presence of the catacombs, no tall buildings can be built in this section of Paris.

The catacombs are actually one of the city's many museums. The official name is *l'Ossuaire Municipal.* During World War II, Parisian members of the French Resistance used the tunnel system, and German soldiers established an underground bunker in the catacombs below *Lycée Montaigne,* a high school in the 6th *arrondissement..*

Starting in 1786, stacks and stacks of bones were placed underground to make more room in the above-ground cemeteries, which were filled to overflowing, in part from the many years of plagues. If you want to read a fascinating piece of historic fiction on this topic, pick up a copy of **PURE** by Andrew Miller. It tells the interesting and gruesome story of *Les Innocents,* the very large cemetery near *Les Halles.* We have walked many of the streets highlighted in the book.

The Catacombs

The catacombs were on our bucket list of places to see in Paris, so one afternoon in our third year, we decided to explore this novelty.

"Are you sure you want to do this?" Bernie asked, almost like he knew something I didn't.

"Of course, I want to do this. Is there some reason you don't want to go?" I asked curiously.

"No, not really," Bernie replied, "I've just read about it and know that it's going to be . . . different."

"Well, we can't come to Paris and **not** see something as famous as this," I added without any hesitancy.

As we approached the street façade, it was not what I was expecting. I was surprised that it was so minimal with a quiet, small entryway. We purchased our tickets and read the first ominous sign: a warning that once in, we wouldn't be able to exit until the very end. Hmmm, in other words, we were trapped! Then, if that wasn't enough, there was a second sign warning about multiple steps inside. That was no big deal to us, given our healthy dose of apartment steps. We crept along a narrow passageway and started down, down, down steep, spiral steps which seemed like they would never end. I held on to the close sides as I inched my way down, thinking—what the heck?! It got darker and darker until finally we were enveloped by underground tunnels full of neatly arranged bones in every direction, **about six million of them**!

Bleary lights dangled from the ceiling, coupled with an eerie silence. Heads of skeletons, femurs, and tibias were grouped together in precise, artistic arrangement, I suppose to show reverence for the departed and to conserve space. We were pretty fascinated for the first twenty minutes or so, but the tunnels of bones went on and on in endless repetition. I began to wonder how people with claustrophobia could ever survive this outing! Occasionally, we turned into small side tunnels but discovered that they led to nothing new; we read most of the historic notes posted along the path that told which cemetery was represented by what group of bones. We walked for almost ninety minutes and the scenery never changed! The creepiest part for me was the slow drip, drip, drip of some unknown liquid from overhead.

"Bernie, what is that?" I said with horror as a big splat hit the top of my forehead and dribbled down.

"Oh, it's just water, leaking through the old mines," Bernie insisted.

"Right!" I said with doubt, "then why is it so thick? I'm sure it's a body fluid of some sort!"

The large viscous splats continued as we walked along, somehow finding only my head and never Bernie's!

I found the catacomb excursion fascinating; however, having done it twice, I have no desire to do it again. There is a reverence about it, and I hope I haven't sounded too flippant. Oddly enough, this outing was at the top of my son's "to-see" list when he visited. Definitely unique to Paris, it is one of the most bizarre memories in our repertoire!

You know you're in Paris...

* If thirty people are in line to buy a cone of *Berthillon* ice cream in fifty-degree weather.
* If the street cleaners spray you down along with the sidewalk.
* If the street toilets look very good after a long walk!
* If the restaurant toilettes are down or up twenty-five steps!
* When no one pays any attention to the stop lights and crosses the street at will.
* If a Parisian on the street comes up to you and says, "Do you need some help?"
* If the clerks in the store playfully try to determine if you're French or American.
* If there is no driver on your subway train!
* If the same two homeless ladies are arguing out on the street. They may have been there for years!
* If there's a dog sitting next to you at dinner.
* If the sun is still dancing on the *Seine* at nine thirty in the evening.
* If people are still eating lunch at four o'clock and dinner at ten.
* If the expressway along the river is closed for *Paris Plages*.
* If no one but you offers a coin to a violin player on the subway.
* If all the church bells are ringing on Sunday morning, calling people to mass.
* If the beautiful green grapes are surprisingly full of seeds!
* If you must bring your own bags to the grocery store or pay for *les sacs*.

- When it seems that all the young people under thirty are smoking.
- When all the grocery store shelves are empty by eight o'clock—truly.
- If elementary children are listening intently to a teacher or grandmother explaining great works of art at a museum.
- When the *pompiers* (firemen) are the most handsome young men around.
- When a ten-year old child sitting next to you orders escargot or steak tartare!
- If the subways are packed like sardines on July 14, Bastille Day.
- If the weather is suddenly the opposite of what it was two minutes ago.
- If the horses from *La Garde Républicaine* go clomping by your window.
- If there is *Café Gourmand* on the menu. (bite-sized desserts with coffee)
- If the waiters are shouting, "*J'arrive!*" (I'm coming.)
- If you're the only people in the restaurant at seven thirty in the evening.
- If you can sit at a café for hours for the price of an *espresso*.

CHAPTER 9

Strolling in Paris

Flâner à Paris

⟶᧶

**If you have ever walked in Paris, you will see that
Paris will ever walk in your memories!**

– MEHMET MURAT ILDAN

WE URGE YOU TO FORGO a touristy temptation like *La Conciergerie* or even a *Seine* river cruise and instead invest that time in a stroll. For one thing, a stroll is free. It's perfect for couples; it can be done in any kind of weather, at any time of day or night, and from wherever you are in Paris. It's not as dramatic or as publicized as other Paris attractions, and in that sense, Bernie and I think strolling is overlooked and underrated by many Paris visitors. That's why we've dedicated an entire chapter to this beautiful Paris experience.

Strolling is to Paris as delicate lace is to lingerie. It's the exquisite finery, the perfect stitching on the finest cloth. *"Les Flâneurs"* or strollers dot the majestic sidewalks and parks of Paris's loveliest areas. Like a mother cradling her baby, Paris wraps *les flâneurs* in her gentle grasp.

Lovers want their time together to last forever, to never change, to be written upon their hearts; and a stroll is their perfect venue. I have already referenced my first stroll with Bernie along the *Seine* near *Notre Dame* on our initial visit. I was goggle-eyed and on sensory overload, but I have never forgotten the intimate thrill of that evening, hand in hand, smelling and sensing the river as the shimmering lights reflected like dancing ballerinas on the water.

Strolling allows love the room it craves to expand and deepen. It's why so many lovers wish to come back; it's why Paris is so difficult to leave; it's why movies like *Casablanca* croon that "we'll always have Paris." Lovers love to stroll because strolling has no focus other than seeing the brightest tilt of the earth—the beauty, the art, the romance, the emotion. It loathes schedule, pace, staccato rhythm, and end destinations. Strolling begets the quiet moments, the glimpses of history, the changing of seasons, the nostalgia of great writers, and the struggle of artists. It gives pause over the pigeons, the gargoyles, the narrow *rues,* the massive doors dressed in bright blues and reds, laden with ornate ironwork or art nouveau carvings. Modern-day strolling evokes the ages, all the feast that Paris has to offer.

Couples, especially older couples who reside in Paris today, still stroll, arm in arm, along the lovely boulevards of *Saint-Germain-des-Prés* and *l'Avenue des Champs Elysées*. The women are dressed in *Chanel* suits and *Ferragamo* shoes; the men, in neatly tucked ascots of silk and cashmere sweaters, perhaps hold-overs from bygone days but still oozing with chic panache. For a fleeting moment as they pass, you see the epitome of style for which Parisians are so well known and for which some lament a recent demise. It's touching to watch and wonder who these strollers are and what their lives may have represented—about Paris, about change, about the tangle of their personal sagas.

For Bernie and me, strolling has taught us to cherish each other's presence without any appointed rendezvous. And that is pure Paris at its best, simply the joy of being together. We surprise ourselves at how a drab, uneventful day can become energized and unforgettable by falling into strolling mode.

Strolling is not typical walking. Walking has a destination in mind, a determined pace, a thought of what's at the end point rather than what's along the way. Walking is also an exercise ritual practiced for calorie burn. Strolling is a lollygag meandering with no focus, an eagerness to discover surprises, and an openness for starts and stops to happen without regard to the clock.

Bernie and I love our slow, easy mornings with the sounds of a city waking up—church bells ringing, garbage being rolled away, people bustling to get their flaky *croissant* and *café au lait*. Eventually, I put on my tour guide hat, and we begin the daily dialogue about what we're going to do. Is it a new museum, a lunch out, a cemetery, a new area or *arrondissement* we've never been to, a shopping destination, a *pique-nique*?

We think we know where we're going, but often find that the best-laid plans in Paris don't materialize exactly as we had hoped. Strolls tend to boil up to the surface as directions are slightly askew, the address is difficult to find, or the write-up that sounded so good does not deliver. *It's what happens between the lines that can be so delicious.* So not to worry—just put one foot out the door and the adventure begins!

If strolling alone as a couple intimidates you, arrange for walking tours from some of the great guides in Paris. For the *Marais* district, we recommend a former New Yorker turned Francophile named Richard Nahem. Just Google him at his blog site, *ipreferparis.net*. He's our neighbor and now good friend, and we think you would find him delightful. If you whip up the courage to go it alone, keep a good street map handy, also a subway map, and remember that street addresses are sometimes out of order. **And ask for help** if you need it.

Surely, by now, you're not surprised when I say that Bernie is the perfect *flâneur*! I trust him to keep me safe wherever we go, on paths both known and unknown. We laugh at ourselves as we remember that in Paris, we really don't have a care in the world. No one is looking for us or expecting anything of us. And if we screw up, no big deal. What a wonderful freedom!

The rest of this chapter is devoted to six of our favorite strolls selected mainly for newcomers to Paris who are staying for a brief period. These can't be missed! There are other suggestions at the end of the chapter for return visits.

STROLL #1: *LA RUE DES ROSIERS*
La Rue des Rosiers, the Street of the Rose Bushes, is the heart of Paris's oldest Jewish quarter in the center of the *Marais* district. And yes, it is lined with

beautiful trees and rose bushes. In this district, "gay bars rub shoulders with falafel cafés, kosher restaurants, synagogues and prayer rooms. Its labyrinthine streets have been home to Jews on and off since the 13th century."[3] There are chic clothing shops, shoe shops, Jewish bakeries, and Middle Eastern food all along the route. *Sacha Finkelsztajn* pastry shop is famous for its apple strudel and cheesecake. If you like *falafel*, this street has several famous walk-up storefronts which will not disappoint—offering take-out—all quite popular and sometimes with long queues. Occasionally, you can catch a trio or quartet singing Jewish folk ballads in the street. There's even a bookstore full of volumes on Jewish history and original Jewish art. A local favorite restaurant is *Chez Marianne* with Middle-Eastern fare.

As you leave the street, it dead ends into *rue du Vieille Temple* (Street of the Old Temple) with quaint restaurants and a people-watching heaven. Grab a table at one of the sidewalk cafes, nurse a glass of wine or a *Kronenbourg 1664* (Alsatian beer), and enjoy yourselves for a few hours. A delightful shop a block off *la rue des Rosiers* which had gorgeous fabrics from all over the world closed a couple of years ago. The owners published a commemorative book called *La Bonne Renommée* (The Good Reputation) for their customers tracing their exotic merchandise through the years. Unfortunately, these mom-and-pop shops, decades old, are disappearing and, along with them, some of the charm of the *Marais* district. The owners are ageing out, and their children are not interested in assuming the proprietorships. It's changing the character of the area; sadly, we wish for time to stand still.

Bernie and I love this area and are drawn to it every trip. It's also one of the favorite strolls to share with our company. Remember, no Saturday strolls here as everything is closed for the Jewish Sabbath, but Sundays are usually abuzz with activity. The Orthodox Jews are noticeably visible in their black suits, black hats, skull caps, untrimmed beards, and sidecurls or *payots* which stand out at first, but after a while, are hardly noticed. The French share a sad destiny in this area for their aid in the deportation of Jewish children while Paris was under Nazis occupation. To learn more about this period in Parisian

---

3   Willsher, Kim. "Jewish People in the French Capital Live in the Shadow of Hatred." *The Guardian,* March 5, 2011.

history, read *Sarah's Key,* by Tatiana de Rosnay. You can even locate (as we did) the actual apartment where Sarah's brother was hidden away from the Nazis and eventually left to die. Sarah returned to the apartment with her key after escaping from a concentration camp, but it was too late to save her little brother. There is a lovely memorial park near the Eiffel Tower to honor the children who were lost in the tragic round-up at the *Velodrome d'Hiver,* described in this book, which was made into a popular movie of the same name.

The memorial of the *Velodrome d'Hiver*

One quick story. *Chez Marianne* is a kosher restaurant and local favorite, and we have eaten there several times with much enjoyment. The last and final time was with my son and daughter-in-law, who were visiting in May of 2008. It was very warm for Paris, and perhaps the buffet was left out a little too long in warm temperatures. (That's what the doctor said!) At any rate, I became deathly sick, spoiling some of the visit and requiring a trip to the emergency room. That bad memory has kept us from returning to the restaurant, but we always enjoy strolling the area. Two years ago, a friend told us about a hidden park down an alleyway, right before the *falafel* shops. Who would have ever believed such a lovely, secluded spot was a block off this crazy maze of activity? It's perfect for eating your *pique-nique* or kosher meal. Seek out this hideaway!

STROLL #2: *L'AVENUE DES CHAMPS ELYSÉES*

Truly the grandest of the grand boulevards in Paris is *Les Champs*. Please no *m* or *p* or *s* in the pronunciation for fear you may sound like an unschooled American! It's pronounced "Le Shahn" for short, with only the slightest hint of the *n*. Lined on both sides with wonderfully coiffed plane trees (a type of sycamore), *l'Avenue des Champs Elysées* could be called the heartbeat of Paris. If it's happening anywhere in the city, it will be happening here. From *Le Tour de France* to movie premieres with Leonardo DiCaprio, to special parades with heart-pounding music, to commemorative war memorial services at *l'Arc de Triomphe*, to the *Bastille* Day parade—we've crafted some of our very special memories here.

L'Avenue des Champs Elysées

On just a regular day, if nothing else is on our itinerary, we may decide to stroll up and down, beginning at the Franklin Roosevelt subway station off Line 1, walking all the way up to the *Arc*, and back down the other side. (And, perhaps you may want to take a deep breath and walk up to the top of the *Arc* for another amazing view of Paris. At the base of the *Arc* are lists of generals who fought for Napoleon. Look for a General Verdier, no kin to Bernie!)

As we stroll, we never know where we may stop, what new surprise we may find, or what new side street may lure us. The sidewalks are thick with humanity from all over the world, with glimpses of odd dress and snippets of foreign expressions as we snake our way through the crowds. There is no lack of good, but very expensive, places to eat. Just a soft drink can easily cost eight to ten dollars! But at least once, indulge and sit out at one of the sidewalk venues that line the avenue, especially when the weather is nice. Jump in and out of the shops, mostly ready-to-wear. One of our favorite stores closed a couple of years ago, the *Virgin* Megastore, which was home to the Bank of America back in the 1970s. The plated vault downstairs is still there, as is the grand staircase. I have read that the space has been declared an architectural landmark, and cannot be modified.

Don't miss the automobile showrooms right on the main thoroughfare—Renault, Peugeot, Toyota, Mercedes. They are unlike anything we have in America, displaying the latest sports car crazes and engineering feats, surrounded by multiple "**Do Not Touch**" signs. They are also a great place for a clean restroom, and one even has a restaurant upstairs.

The old shopping arcades called *passages* also line *Les Champs*—designer clothes, shoes, perfume, art work, a good restaurant or two—all expensive, all purely Paris. Then there's the *Lido*, an upscale version of *Le Moulin Rouge*. It's a must-see at least once! Make your reservation right on the street. Next, put on your rich airs and walk into *Louis Vuitton* along with the masses. Its multiple stories are full of chic fashion accessories at ridiculous prices! Maybe you can actually buy that €800 purse. The street-side windows are notorious for creative displays; be sure to snap some photos. If you go all the way to the top floor, you will discover an art museum. You really haven't been to Paris unless you've been to *Louis Vuitton*.

Take a spin off *Les Champs* onto *l'Avenue George V* and discover *l'Hôtel George V* a few blocks down, where Princess Di often stayed. The floral arrangements are extraordinary, and you can have an afternoon aperitif in the Garden Room while you rest your feet.

If you're in Paris during the Christmas holidays, the trees along *Les Champs* are graced with twinkling white lights, and Christmas stalls line the avenue for holiday shopping.

Stroll *l'Avenue des Champs Elysées,* and while you're in Paris make an attempt to pronounce it as the French do—all run together!

Purely Paris

Bernie has admitted to a street theft on *Les Champs* many years ago, long before he and I met! He was so tired of never seeing his name listed anywhere in America that he went into a phone booth and ripped out two and a half pages from the Paris phonebook, listing all the Verdiers. Hilarious!

STROLL #3: *LE JARDIN DES TUILERIES*

Any trip to Paris must include a trip to the *Louvre*. Between us, Bernie and I have been a dozen times. We either stumble accidentally on some of the same things or find wonderful new surprises. It's a maze of discovery and delights every single trip; I'm not sure that you can ever see **all** that the *Louvre* has to offer.

Despite how much you may research and plan, you will still get lost in the *Louvre's* massive wings. Don't think, as my son did, that all you do is stroll up and down long hallways looking at pieces of artwork hanging on walls. Oh, there's some of that, to be sure. But there is so much more—artifacts from the ancient worlds of Persia, Egypt, and Babylonia; the apartments of Napoleon which are on par with Versailles; Greek and Roman sculptures, and gorgeous pieces of furniture and fine china from the French monarchies.

Don't spoil your trip and go on a Tuesday; the *Louvre* is always closed. The first Sunday of each month, it is free to the public, but we have never been willing to stand in the very long line.

So what does the *Louvre* have to do with our third strolling suggestion? It's the beginning point of one of the grandest strolls in Paris! If you exit up the escalator and out through the glass pyramid, the ancient palace unfolds before your eyes. Turn all the way around and take in the beauty as you imagine daily life here for regal kings and queens.

Walk across the grounds through the *Triump Arch,* and *Le Jardin des Tuileries* opens up as far as you can see. You will cross a busy street of bustling traffic (a la *The Da Vinci Code*), so be very careful.

The gardens start immediately and extend for four long city blocks parallel to *rue de Rivoli* all the way to *La Place de la Concorde* with the Egyptian obelisk. Sunday afternoon is one of the best times to make this stroll and avoid some of the tourists who are hopefully busing on to their next destination. Take a rest in the classic, green lawn chairs which are the trademark of any Parisian park. On a busy day, they will be hard to snatch. If you're lucky to be here in spring or summer, the gardens will be alive with manicured, blooming color. If in the fall, you will see a different array of flowers. Even winter will have its special shade of gray—Paris in sepia, still beautiful in its own way. All parks and gardens in Paris are unpaved. The walkways are a fine sandy grit which gets a little exasperating in sandals. It's one of those nit-picks that get to me. If you like sand under your toes, you'll love it.

Jardin des Tuileries

Meander, meander, meander. Stop for refreshment or ride the huge Ferris wheel in the summer. Listen to the buzz of conversation and laughter. Sail a boat in the big lake in the center. Walk along the outside of the gardens as well as the main inside promenade. There are nooks and crannies everywhere with statues that are centuries old. Surely there will be an artist or two performing on a violin, maybe even an accordion, or the famous bird man feeding the chickadees. A mime may entertain you and all the children. For a coin, you can take his picture!

At the end of your stroll, save time to stop at *Musée de L'Orangerie*, a lovely art museum which showcases the massive water lily tableaus of Claude Monet. They are breathtakingly beautiful and better to us than going to *Giverny,* Monet's home with the famous lily pad ponds. The museum houses an impressive collection of fine art downstairs. Save at least an hour for this part of your stroll, and then finish at *La Place de la Concorde.* It's a challenge to negotiate the huge traffic circle but worth it to see the Egyptian obelisk up close.

Monet's water lily mural in
Musée de L'Orangerie

What a stroll! You have seen one of the world's largest and most treasured art museums, the only one in perfect architectural alignment with *l'Arc de Triomphe*. You have walked the gardens of kings, tasted a sample of Parisian camaraderie, seen Monet's brilliant watercolors, and ended with nearly getting run over in a traffic circle. Now you are a true Parisian!

Stroll #4: The River *Seine*

If *l'Avenue des Champs Elysées* is the heartbeat of Paris, the River *Seine* is the soul. It not only separates the city into the well-known Right Bank/Left Bank sections, it also represents the one enduring constant about Paris. Everything has changed around it—economics, fashion, transportation, religion, politics, food, housing, and social behavior. But the river remains as it has always been. It moves with certainty—sometimes raging, sometimes gently flowing—shimmering and projecting the glorious light across ancient buildings, bouncing sunbeams in lovers' eyes, teeming with both commerce and tourists, and playing host to magnificent bridges.

The soul of a place is the core of its existence, the unpretentious purity, the element which defines and gives meaning. To Bernie and me, the River *Seine* is such a symbol. It's alive, breathing, moving, feeling. Lovers kiss, hold hands, argue, stroll, propose marriage, sing songs, drink wine, laugh, cry—all along this one mighty waterway. It even spawned the birth of Paris or *Lutetia* ages ago. It has seen centuries of change—floods, disease, war, near starvation, and brutal hatred. It could tell all but doesn't. It holds the secrets, the joys, the disappointments, the disruption with dignity and honor.

At least once while you're in Paris, find a spot on the river and start to stroll. Stand on the bridges at all times of the day and night and soak up the messages of the river. We prefer the area around the islands of *Ile St. Louis* and *Ile de la Cité*, but there are numerous other wonderful areas around the *La Tour Eiffel, Le Musée d'Orsay, Quai Branly*, or *La Place de la Bastille*. Take your lover by the hand and stroll a while up top; then take the steps down to the lower level where you can feel the rush of the river. Twilight is our favorite time on *Pont Marie*, our good-bye spot. But more on that later.

The Majestic River *Seine*

Bigger and better than any of us, this mighty river will become your connecting symbol to Paris and to the person with whom you shared its majesty. Why do you think the controversial lovelocks along the bridges have been so popular? They were the ultimate love symbol: two lovers' names plus the date written on a padlock, hooked to one of the bridges, and the key tossed into the river! Everlasting, unbreakable love—How romantic was that? Until. . . it became too much of a good thing. The locals raised such a voice of protest that now authorities are removing the heavy locks from the bridges, which were never meant to handle the extra tonnage. Despite the controversy, lovers return, and the river still oozes its romantic charm.

STROLL #5: *LE VIADUC DES ARTS/LE PORT DE PARIS*

We read about *Le Viaduc des Arts,* the Viaduct of Arts, and realized that it was in our neighborhood, about a fifteen-minute walk from the apartment. We loved it on our first trip and every time after that. It is a nineteenth century viaduct— truly an old railway trellis, a few blocks behind the new opera house at *La Place de la Bastille.* Underneath the viaduct arches are chic shops which house artisans ranging from jewelry makers to furniture craftsmen, many embodying the

French word *atelier* or workshop. After you check out the shops, find the stairway leading up to the park on top where the train traversed, and then enjoy a lovely quiet stroll above the treetops, showcasing stunning views of the architecture of classic Parisian buildings. Bernie and I love to be at eye-level with the penthouse suites! The French are masterful at repurposing their oldest structures in creative, artistic ways, and this one is a masterpiece. Read more about this transformation at: *http://europeforvisitors.com/paris/articles/viaduc-des-arts.htm.*

There are benches along the park offering a rest, a picnic, or a nap. It is never overrun with people and appears to be a lovers' lane of sorts. You can walk easily for about a half mile. Save time to stop at one of the moderately priced restaurants for lunch as you approach or leave the viaduct as Bernie and I always do. A long walk deserves some relaxation and an hour of people-watching!

We did this stroll in 2007, 2008, and again in 2014, and found it still alive and thriving. It's only a small section of a three-mile stroll called the *La Coulée verte* which we walked with some friends in 2015. It's a lovely but LONG stroll in the lush greenness of out-of-the-way Paris. So you have two choices, the shorter version, or, if you're up for it, the longer one, complete with exercise equipment along the way!

Linda at *Le Viaduc des Arts*

As you are leaving and going back toward *La Place de la Bastille,* go left at the opera house toward the river and continue strolling along *Le Port de l'Arsenal,* which is an inland tributary of the *Seine* morphing into *Le Canal Saint-Martin.* It's a magnet for yachts and sailboats with a small park which materializes along the side. There's a waterside bar and restaurant called *Le Grand Bleu* where locals gather for a late afternoon cocktail. (Beware of the waiters here as they can be gruff.) Find a table if you can under the shade trees and enjoy the sun's light as it hits the ancient buildings of *Le Marais.* Trust me, the light is different in Paris. You'll remember that I said so! Cross the pedestrian bridge back over the canal into the *Marais,* or you can continue down, through the locks and eventually end up on the *Seine.* We LOVE this area and have gotten some great photos here.

Le Port de Paris or *Le Port de l'Arsenal*

One funny I must share is from an evening stroll. We watched a presumed prostitute with her prey actually "hooking up" along this route. She was sitting on a three-foot wall, and he was making the best of that angle. Another *Oh là là!* We have pictures of this and witnesses! *C'est Paris, n'est-ce pas?* (It's Paris, isn't it?) All it takes is a good zoom lens.

#6: *LA RUE MOUFFETARD*

Strolling in Paris would not be authentic without some time on the Left Bank. As opposed to the usual well-known strolls along *Boulevard Saint-Germain des Prés* or *Boulevard Saint-Michel*, we have decided to share one that better captures old Paris to us, *rue Mouffetard*. We've been here several times, the first by *Métro* where we could see nothing above ground. Ah, but it was the second time that was magnificent—on foot. We crossed the river down from *Notre Dame* and started up, up, up climbing into the Latin Quarter with our street map, Google app, and our most comfortable shoes. If you decide to do this stroll, be forewarned that it's a steep climb, so take a break by popping into some of the little boutiques, especially the chocolate shops. The tiny *rues* meander until you finally discover *la rue Mouffetard*. If you get tired of the climb, find a taxi stand and ask them to take you to this famous street. Everybody knows it. We like to start at the bottom and walk our way up. Don't go too early or some of the shops will be closed, and don't go on Mondays for the same reason.

There are multiple open-air fruit stands, meat shops, cheese shops, boutiques with beautiful scarves, souvenir shops, ready-to-wear shops and a beehive of locals and voyeurs milling around. This is a great Sunday morning market spot. At the very top is a delightful shady *place* or square. About three-quarters of the way to the top is our favorite alleyway, *rue du Pot-de-Fer*, the street of the iron pot. I love it because it's reminiscent of some of the streets in *Montmartre*. It goes higher and higher toward the hill's crest and is lined on both sides with colorful sidewalk cafés—eye candy with a palette of pastel tablecloths and napkins, all vying to lure you in for a bite of lunch. We haven't found great food along this route, but it is adequate and reasonably priced for a hungry appetite.

La rue du Pot-de-Fer is not wide enough for automobiles—though one day, we did experience someone trying to drive right through it!

"Bernie, don't look now," I gasped as I was taking a bite of my lunch, "but there's a car trying to inch its way down this narrow street. It's coming right at us."

"Oh, my," said Bernie, who was already laughing as the commotion around us heightened.

"*Excusez-moi, madame!*" said the waiter as he hoisted me from my chair right in the middle of my bite. I jumped up and stepped back out of the way.

"*Excusez-moi, monsieur,*" another waiter said to Bernie as he was also up-ended from his chair.

Both the waiters were flustered, angry, but ever polite. With plenty of *oh là là's* under their breaths, they proceeded to feverishly slide tables and chairs away from all the patrons to make room for the obtrusive motorist. After the car had passed, the tables and chairs quickly reappeared, and we continued our meal as though nothing had happened!

This passage is a shortcut to *La Sorbonne* (the famous Parisian university) for students who live nearby. As you are eating, there's no extra charge for the people-watching or the fashion show from the parade of college students, donned in new-age Parisian chic—black leather, short shorts, chains, tats, and rainbow-colored hair.

After you have paid the bill, walk to the crest of *la rue du Pot-de-Fer* and start back down in the direction of the dome of the Pantheon, a must-see on the Left Bank. Let it be your guide, and keep twisting and turning until you reach it. Many famous French citizens are buried in the Pantheon, including Marie Curie, Victor Hugo, and Voltaire. Don't miss the fact that you can go up and outside the dome to experience another breathtaking view of Paris, capturing the river, *Notre Dame*, and, of course, a glimpse of the Eiffel Tower. In 2013, officials discovered that the weight of the massive dome was pushing against the walls of the building. Eventually, it would have come crashing in on itself. The entire structure has been under major restoration by the state of France and has looked like a big ice cream cone from a distance. After years of work, it has reopened ahead of schedule.

Oh yes, one fun thing to find in this same area are the steps from the movie *Midnight in Paris*. Despite years of looking for them in *Montmartre*, we found them here off to the side of the beautiful church, *Saint-Etienne-du-Mont*—at the top of the *place* and across from the Pantheon.

Now your stroll is complete and you can walk down, down, down the hill or find a subway stop. It's a day's worth of bountiful memories, albeit some sore feet!

Appreciate the fact that I have shared only six of our strolls; I started out with twenty-five! There are so many more that are equally delightful: *l'Avenue Foch, Le Jardin du Luxembourg, Parc Monceau, la rue de Bac, Le Jardin d'Acclimatation, la rue Saint-Denis, Les Halles, Parc des Butte Chaumont, l'Esplanade de La Défense*. We hope you have time for all of them, but the point is—become *un flâneur à Paris*!

Purely Paris

One of our most difficult encounters with a taxi cab driver happened in the *place* right across from the Pantheon. We were looking for a rental car location, unaware that it was underground. The cabbie got very testy and refused at first to take us underground to get the car. Finally, he did drive us down into this dungeon, but only after a scary, loud bout of French between Bernie and him. We never used that particular rental location again!

CHAPTER 10

Shopping in Paris

Faire du shopping à Paris

Paris is a heaven for all woman's obsessions: hot men, great
chocolates, scrumptious pastries, sexy lingerie, cool clothes but, as
any shoe-o-phile knows, this city is a hotbed of fabulous shoes.

– Kirsten Lobe, *Paris Hangover*

I love to attempt to shop in Paris for two reasons: ignorance and reckless abandon. No matter how badly I bungle things—recall the maternity shop fiasco—no one really knows or cares. I find freedom in that and such unlimited opportunity. My advice: Take plenty of euros, some courage, and hit the streets!

I used to never go shopping alone mainly because of the language barrier; now I do it all the time. It's the perfect way to try my skill at speaking French. I make so many mistakes but find the Parisians very appreciative of my effort. They love to practice their English, so it's a beneficial *tête-à-tête* (head-to-head encounter) and a great method for building self-confidence. Never doubt that the French are just as hesitant and embarrassed about speaking English as we are about speaking French. How comforting that can be when you're out by yourself.

"Where are you going?" Bernie will say.

"I'm not exactly sure, but while you're napping, I'm walking around. And if I'm not back when you wake up, come looking for me!"

So far nothing drastic has happened. I generally stay in *Le Marais* and find boutiques to show Bernie later. He patiently frequents quaint little shops that offer old silverware, children's clothing, housewares, delicatessen products, perfume, shoes, and even women's clothing. He's an attentive, shopping voyeur.

There is so much creativity in the *Marais* commerce; you never know what to expect. For example, steps away from us is a shop called *Thanksgiving,* which has only American food products. They sell Jif peanut butter, Aunt Jemima syrup, Captain Crunch cereal—not that I would purchase any of those, of course, except for the peanut butter. It's nine euros a jar which is over ten dollars! PB & J's are special in Paris.

Shopping for necessities and shopping for pleasure are quite different. The former depends on how desperate you are, and the later depends on your budget. If money is no object, you've come to the right city! If, like Bernie and me, you have to watch your nickels and dimes, shopping especially for pleasure, will be a challenge. I jokingly say to Bernie, "Just give me two hours and three thousand euros, and I will show Parisians the true American spirit!"

All of this fantasy aside, it's so very expensive in Paris—*très, très cher!* The penalty you get in converting dollars to euros affects every meal, every purchase, and every ticket. Depending on how lucky you get during your stay, the exchange rate will generally mean ten to fifty cents more for every dollar you spend. That adds up in a hurry. Learn to do the simple math in your head, or you'll be shocked when you get your credit card bill, not to mention the transaction and conversion fees charged by your credit card company. Just as I'm writing these words, the dollar is now (2015) only a nickel more than the euro. Wonders never cease.

Grocery Stores, Fruit Stands & Other Food Shopping

If you are renting an apartment, shopping for food and life necessities which you didn't have room to pack is probably the first outing you will make. All neighborhoods in Paris have a grocery store nearby. The largest chains are the *G-20, Franprix,* Leader Price, *Carrefour* and *Monoprix.* Keep an eye out for these logos wherever you're staying. The *G-20* and *Franprix* are less expensive than the *Monoprix,* but not as large or as similar to American grocery stores.

Our favorite shopping experience for what we use day-to-day is the *Monoprix* on *rue Saint-Antoine,* except for Bernie's bread! It has everything—make-up, greeting cards, a terrific wine cellar, groceries, fresh fish, dishes, light bulbs, extension cords, exotic cheeses, deli products, lingerie, baby clothes, fashionable ladies' and men's clothing, even pillows! We buy our household items like Saran Wrap, paper towels, napkins, place mats, and detergent here. The prices are reasonable. It's a massive, two-story building and cold as ice downstairs in the grocery area—cold enough to always wear a sweater! We avoid shopping after five o'clock because of long, check-out lines. Locals are leaving work and stopping in for their evening meal purchases. By eight o'clock, the shelves are basically empty!

Bernie and I make a good team grocery shopping together. We even have our own affinity card from the *Monoprix,* where we get discounts on special sale items! Bernie loves it because it makes him feel like he's at home. He gets the wine, other liquor which is sold in the grocery aisles, and the cheese; also his bananas and apricots, as he is particular about those. I get the regular items and the rest of the produce. Milk comes in unrefrigerated boxes, and the bottled water is profuse. We are in and out in under twenty minutes. We pack our own grocery totes because the *Monoprix* charges three cents for each of their plastic bags. (Note: We discovered in 2016 that plastic bags are no longer allowed in Paris. All retailers must convert to paper bags within a given timeframe.) The store provides small roller carts, or you can get a big cart similar to what we have at home for a euro. When you return it, you get your euro back. Before we came over to stay in our apartment the first time, I purchased and packed our own roller cart to push through the streets of Paris. This is what the locals use, but alas, it was heavy, filled half a large suitcase, and eventually was donated to charity.

Oddly enough, the grocery store is the one place where Parisians hustle. There's a frenzy to getting our items out of our push cart, placing the divider between us and the next customer, having the correct change, bagging our items, paying and moving on. It drives me crazy! Bernie gets frustrated because I insist on putting away my money before I move along, and it slows down the process.

"You'll just have to wait a minute!" I say with repeated frustration, "I'm not about to be fumbling with large bills on the streets of Paris. You have to be patient with me since I'm paying with cash."

Once at a neighborhood fruit stand, I pulled out a wad of €20 bills which I had just gotten from the ATM and was severely reprimanded by a clerk.

"*Non, Non, Madame!*" he scolded, as he shook his finger right in my face, gesturing for me to get the money out of sight.

In addition to all the neighborhood grocery stores, we adore the mom-and-pop fruit stands. Prices depend on the neighborhood. What we pay for fruit around the corner from our apartment at *Le Verger St. Paul* is much less expensive than what we would pay on *Ile Saint- Louis,* for example. Cherries and apricots are everywhere during the months of June and July, but remember not to touch the fruit. The *verger* or market clerk will select for you; you simply point to your choice and order the amount— "*un demi kilo, s'il vous plaît*" (half a kilogram, please). Yes, it's confusing, but you will catch on. The clerk will walk the ticket to the cashier. After you have paid, the clerk will hand the fruit to you with a polite "*Merci.*"

We also love the traveling markets which ramp up once a week in almost all neighborhoods. Just observe or ask around for which day of the week your market appears. Our day is Wednesday. It's amazing how they are thrown up and torn down with such speed. Watch out in the summer for items that may not be adequately refrigerated. Some bad shrimp sent me to the hospital! These markets are fascinating and colorful to walk through, and occasionally, I have found a bargain or two.

Food shopping will not be complete without a stop at a Parisian sensation called *Picard's* which sells frozen, gourmet French food that can be either defrosted or microwaved. (Hail to the working woman!) There are multiple locations throughout Paris, but the one we use is right across the river on the Left Bank at the end of *Saint-Germain-des-Prés.* I can **cook** all the exquisite French delights like *cordon bleu* or *baba au rhum* (a small yeast cake saturated in rum, and sometimes filled with whipped cream or pastry cream) with a stop at this one store. It seems almost heretical but a great way to impress company—ha!

One final word about an *epicerie* at *Le Bon Marche*, one of Paris's famous old department stores on the Left Bank. Bernie and I were looking for pickled garlic, which is served at the bar in *Le Train Bleu,* and the waiter told us we could find it here. This *epicerie* or gourmet grocery store is a separate massive section of the department store and a fabulous food experience. It is similar to the basement at Harrods in London. It's Fresh Market, Earth Fare, and Whole Foods all rolled into one spacious, artistic expression of the finest that Paris has to offer in gastronomies. Take plenty of euros, some dawdling time, and enjoy. It's a fun outing whether you intend to purchase anything or not.

SUNDAY/ SPECIALTY MARKETS

La Place de la Bastille has a Sunday morning market which we love, love, love! It extends four or five city blocks. Go—if for no other reason than to see and hear the fruit vendors, especially toward the closing hours as they barter and bark out their bargain prices. You will find not only a huge array of fruits and veggies but also meat, fish, cheeses, wine, imported clothing, jewelry, flea market items, shoes, scarves, art work, umbrellas, gift items, you name it. It's a great Sunday morning outing followed by an omelet and *chocolat chaud* at the closest sidewalk café. It may be a novelty for us tourists, but it's a regular outing for resident Parisians who count on great variety and good prices.

The Sunday Market at *La Place de la Bastille*

Marché Beauvau, Place d'Aligre is another wonderful market—older, covered, and hard to find. It's less than a mile behind *L'Opera Bastille* and is open daily, not just on Sundays. It's colorful and fun, but with a smaller variety of non-food items. The interior section has meats, cheeses, breads, sausages, olives, and baked goods. Like so many venues in Paris, it is basically closed during the month of August because of *les vacances* (vacation).

Don't fret about finding these exact spots. Wherever you are in Paris, **there will be a market**! And it will be a fun experience.

THE OLD FABRIC DISTRICT

If you walk straight down from *Le Sacré Coeur* atop *Montmartre* on the winding pathway into the park below, you will intersect busy streets at the bottom which lead to the fabric district on the left. If you're into beautiful fabrics or like to sew, don't miss this. Floor after floor in store after store are rolls and rolls of fabrics, lace, and sewing notions. Many Parisians still make their own clothes, especially wedding gowns for their families. These are classic stores, *grand magasins,* from the turn of the century with oiled hardwood floors and large gated elevators. Depending on your level of interest, you can spend hours.

I must admit that this is not Bernie's favorite, but he allows me the fun. Sometimes, we split up. I shop or look; he works a Sudoku puzzle at a nearby café and has an afternoon aperitif. It's a great compromise.

PARIS DISCOUNT

In our *Marais* neighborhood is a store on *rue de Rivoli* that is just like a TJ Maxx. It's two blocks down from the merry-go-round at the *Saint-Paul Métro* stop, on the opposite side of the street. *Paris Discount* has brand-name merchandise for greatly reduced prices, and there are locations throughout Paris. Let's say you arrive at your apartment, and your pillows are horrible. Or you need nice but affordable dishes, a bath mat, or even a lamp. Stores like this are the place to go when you don't want to overspend, knowing that you will likely leave the purchase behind. Different items are available on different days, depending on their incoming shipments. We duck into this store at least once a week just to see if there are any bargains.

LOCAL *BOULANGERIES/PÂTISSERIES*

These are neighborhood-driven, mostly locally owned, and everywhere in Paris. The *boulangerie* (bakery) bakes bread of every shape, size, and texture plus all kinds of sweets—cakes, pastries, and cookies. The *pâtisserie* (cake shop) does virtually the same thing. You'll find the one that suits you best. In *Le Marais*, our favorite is *Miss Manon,* mostly because we can see it from our apartment window. As I mentioned earlier, I can't tell the difference in the bread or the croissants or the pastries from one shop to the next, but the Parisians certainly can. They are quick to tell you which is their favorite and more emphatically which is not! I can ogle and drool for hours at the sheer artistry of the pastries.

SHOPPING CENTERS OR MALLS

Paris has its share of big malls, but often, they are hidden away in places you'd never suspect, reached via massive escalators going down into the bowels of the earth. It's amazing how the French carve out layered space. These malls are where regular folks with regular incomes do much of their shopping for clothing. One in particular is *Le Forum des Halles* in the area near *Les Halles,* the famous historic meat and food market which was shut down for hygienic reasons years ago. It was notoriously famous for its French onion soup, served at any hour of the day. Some Parisians have never gotten over its demise. And many attempts to refurbish the area have been short-lived. A new, totally modern "monstrosity" is going up right now to include an ultra-modern subway station and shopping mall with a target date of 2017. Hopefully, we'll live to see it! I personally don't think its contemporary style fits into such a classically historic area, and I already fear I won't like it. These shopping centers are not spread out with huge parking lots as in America, but rather jam-packed in consolidated spaces that can feel downright eerie at times. They're overrun with shoppers and sprinkled with pickpockets; so choose your times wisely if you decide to make the journey "down under" by escalator or moving sidewalks. I did just read that a section of this is now open, a year in advance.

Les Quatre Temps or Four Seasons is in the modern section of Paris called *La Défense*, located at the end of Line 1 on the *Métro*. At the exit, follow the signs carefully to shopping or *Quatre Temps*. It's a complicated beehive of craziness. Prior to entering the mall, you will find yourself in a huge transportation hub with subways and the *RER* (Paris rails). If you get confused, just stop and ask until you find the shopping area. It's massive and covers five floors with 250 shops. The top floor is a food court along with a movie theatre. We like to eat lunch at *Le Hippopotamus* or *Le Hippo* as the French call it. The food is Americanized, I must admit, but once in a while, it's good to have some chips and salsa, *mais oui* (but yes)? There's even a Starbucks if you feel like betrayal. I'm pretty sure you will get lost in this mall, but just relax and enjoy. The higher the floor, the more expensive the shops. Make certain you go outside on the top floor and see the massive, modern Arch which is in perfect alignment with *L'Arc de Triomphe*. This area is the Manhattan of Paris with towering skyscrapers, reflecting pools, fountains, flowers, and a carousel for the children. Highly impressive! As you leave, you will need your ticket to get out. Follow the signs with the big encircled M, *Métro* symbol, take Line 1 again, but in the opposite direction to *Château de Vincennes*.

Bernie and I have funny stories getting out of here. I'll pass my ticket through the automated gate, and then when he tries, his will not work. I'm looking at him through the Plexiglas barriers saying, "Oh dear, I'll see you at the apartment." He has to go buy a ticket that works. It's a pain but no reason to panic. Whenever these bizarre things happen in Paris, take a deep breath, smile, and walk up to a well-chosen stranger and say, *"Excusez-moi, monsieur ou madame. Parlez vous anglais?"* ("Excuse me, sir or madam. Do you speak English?") Almost without fail, they do and will help you. Trust us!

Carrousel du Louvre is another hidden shopping mecca underneath the *Louvre*. It is accessed from Subway Line 1 and offers some good shopping prior to your visit to the museum. It is all on one floor, and they cater to Americans, I think, with shops like Swarovski, Swatch, Apple, L'Occitane, all popular in the United States. It's a pleasant experience and offers you a chance to see the base of the famous, inverted pyramid, made so popular in *The Da Vinci Code*. And on a hot day, it's air-conditioned!

ANTIQUES AND *BROCANTE (* FLEA MARKET ITEMS*)*

Just as there are local markets in every area of Paris, there's certainly a plethora of antique shops to entice you. Many are clustered on the Left Bank. If you are a serious antique connoisseur, I would search the web. I have noticed that often the shops are not open during typical hours. Many are by appointment only.

Brocante is the French word for flea market items, and generally their shows move around through Paris frequently. They are like flea markets in the United States—some junk, some really authentic bargains, antique jewelry, silver flatware, china, linens, clothing, and much more. I'm not big on flea market shopping, but if you are, you will not be disappointed. Usually prior to the shows' arrival, there is ample pre-promotion with banners which hang across the narrow *rues* citing dates, times, and exact locations. There is a large *brocante* show every year at *Le Village Saint-Paul* in June and sometimes one at *La Place de la Bastille*. I have purchased a very nice necklace of *lapis lazuli* as my one and only *brocante* extravaganza.

There is one flea market you must not miss—*Le Marché aux Puces.* (Subway: *La Porte de Clignancourt*) It's a full day's worth of shopping mania and amazing meandering. Don't be in a hurry, and take note that the area is only open on the weekends, spilling over to Mondays. Typical of Paris, it doesn't crank up until around eleven o'clock. The crowd is smaller on Mondays as this is the day primarily for local dealers to scout out new items.

Don't go on a rainy day because the shops are like open-air tunnels; you will be walking outside half the time. The tiny cubbies are graced with ivy and grape vines in row after row, haphazardly meshed together by a tangle of electrical wires, awnings, and outdoor displays. It's very easy to get lost, turned around, and hard to find the exact entrance and exits. Bathrooms are few!

When you first exit the subway, it's quite a long walk through a barrage of venders from around the world, hawking their products in your face. Be aware that this preliminary section is **not** *Le Marché aux Puces*. Some folks get caught in this and never go beyond it. The flea market is several blocks farther down to the left, beyond the overpass. After you are truly inside, you can find gorgeous antique linens, old LPs, old postcards, old magazines, pottery, retro clothing, furniture, pure junk, trinkets from cheap to exquisite (Limoges), silver, rugs, and the list goes on and on. It is absolutely one of the most iconic outings ever and is known throughout the world as a Paris *Oh là là*!

The surrounding area is not so good, and you will immediately see a noticeable, unpleasant difference from nicer parts of Paris—lots of litter and few good places to eat. We tried the one little restaurant inside the flea market on our last visit, and all I can say is **OMG!** It was most definitely old Paris. One in our group unknowingly ordered intestines—literally! Two old divas were singing opera amid the Christmas tinsel streaming across the ceiling. (It was July.) They demanded a tip afterward, one of the few times this has happened to us in Paris. But it was all in great fun, even the bathrooms in the alley. Once here was probably enough, even for us—ha!

The flea market vendors will barter a little, but don't insult them by starting out too low. Most speak pretty good English (if they want to). Unlike the Grand Bazaar in Istanbul, the French vendors are not pushy at all. They allow you to browse and enjoy their shops. Be sure to say, "*Bonjour, madame, monsieur* or *mademoiselle*" upon entering.This will get you started on the right foot. Upon departure say, "*Au revoir, merci*! *Bonne journée*" (Good-bye, thanks, have a nice day).

Well-informed antique hunters and flea market aficionados will have a field day here. *Le Marché aux Puces* will be a memory!

P.S. They ship, even big pieces like furniture.

Our Favorite Gift Shops

Just a quick mention of a few gift shops to visit while in Paris. There are dozens more but these are some of our favorites.

At *Le Louvre* on the ground floor just past security is both a wonderful bookstore known for its array of art postcards and a separate gift shop with classy items relating to art, sculpture, history, children's books and toys, and souvenirs. I have one friend who challenges me to bring her a certain type of art postcard every year, and this is the place!

Le Palais Garnier, the old opera house, has a gift shop which opened a few years ago and is adjacent to their outdoor café. If you are looking for unique souvenirs or gift items to take to friends at home, spend thirty minutes here. Most of the items (purses, scarves, jewelry, slippers, purse holders, and dishes) have to do with ballet and theatre, as you might imagine; but they are a step up from the mundane and surprisingly affordable by Paris standards.

Petrossians, complete with boutique and restaurant, is a Paris treasure and located near *Les Invalides* on *rue de l'Université.* It is best known for its caviar, but we love to purchase gift tins of chocolate cognac candy— divinely different and a special delight for really good friends back home. Beware, however, because this shop will do major damage to your credit cards.

Fauchons is located at *La Place de la Madeleine* in one of the high-rent areas of Paris, and is well known by both Parisians and tourists. It has an eye-popping, enticing array of candies, *macarons*, and pastries packaged with Parisian panache. Guys will love the prestigious wine cellar downstairs, and there's a chic restaurant upstairs with scrumptious luncheon selections. Plan to eat first, shop after, and relish in the creative merchandising. Again, hold tight to your pocketbooks; you will be tempted to purchase a little of everything. Bernie and I love this spot because we have memories of eating here with his French cousins and other friends.

Ladurée is the original creator of the Parisian *macaron*, dating back to 1862. If you like *macarons*, this is your spot. This French cookie with sweet goodness between two meringue wafers is nothing like the coconut variety we have in the States. There are multiple locations all over the city, but probably the most famous and most crowded is the location on *Les Champs*. Many contain very nice tearooms for a totally French bite of lunch. The lines are long!

DEPARTMENT STORES OR *LES GRANDS MAGASINS*

A visit to Paris for more than three or four days demands a visit to at least one of *les grands magasins*. There are several to choose from—*Les Galeries Lafayette, Le Printemps, Le Bon Marché* or *Le BHV Marais (Bazar de l'Hôtel de Ville*—Since 2015, the *BHV* has changed its name and is called *BHV Marais*). Let me draw a frame of reference for our American readers. The *BHV Marais* is the Belk or JC Penney; *Bon Marché* is Macy's; *Au Printemps* is Saks or Nordstrom's; and *Les Galeries Lafayette* is Neiman Marcus. If money is no object for you, get lost in the designer floor of *Les Galeries Lafayette* for exquisite, designer clothes beyond imagination and price.

All of these have points of distinction—for example, the food sections in both *Bon Marché* and *Les Galeries Lafayette* or the basement hardware section in the *BHV Marais*. Most have delightful spots for lunch (not the food courts!), and the view atop *Les Galeries Lafayette* is one of the best in Paris. The *Bon Marché* is the only one on the Left Bank, and the *BHV Marais*, of course, is in *Le Marais*. The other two are just behind the *Palais Garnier* in the heart of the city.

I must admit that my favorite is *Les Galeries Lafayette* because of its famous domed ceiling, made of stained glass. When you walk in, you must immediately move to the center of the store, start looking up and prepare to gasp!

If your visit coincides with any of the holidays such as Easter or Christmas, check out the storefront windows. Just like *Louis Vuitton*, you will overload your camera snapping photos of these lush, window dressings. From bicycles to train tunnels, alligators to safaris, merry-go-rounds to Ferris wheels, the creativity abounds. Bernie has spent hours taking snapshots of store windows at all hours of the day. The trick is to somehow avoid the reflections—which ain't easy! What fun we've had at this endeavor.

The stained-glass dome at *Les Galeries Lafayette*

SPECIALTY SHOPS

To reiterate, Paris wouldn't be Paris without the dozens of specialty shops, locally owned sometimes for many years by the same family. Within a couple of blocks in all directions of our apartment are two cheese shops, three chocolate shops, two wine shops, a meat shop or *boucherie*, a full delicatessen called *Sanglier*, three bakeries, three flower shops, a half dozen shoe stores, an elite shop for men's clothing, dozens of ladies' dress shops, a *vaissellerie* (dishes), a maternity shop, a linen shop, a bookstore, and three hair salons. You get the picture!

DESIGNER AND BOUTIQUE SHOPPING

The hot spots for *haute couture* (high fashion) are *rue Saint-Honoré, Place Vendôme, Avenue Montaigne,* around *la Place de la Madeleine,* and as mentioned *Louis Vuitton* on *Les Champs.* If you can afford a $1,000 pocketbook or a $3,000 suit, these are your destinations. Or you can do as we do, and just have fun looking. Bernie is a dear as he enjoys this as much as I do. We dress up a little, act like we are rich, and see if we can pull it off. Usually, we do! If you're near the *Place Vendôme,* step into the Ritz and have a drink at the Hemingway Bar after five-thirty in the evening. Three years ago, the going fare for a mixed drink was €35 or about $42! In 2014, the Ritz was closed for a total make-over and due to reopen in 2016. A recent fire on the top floor has set that back, but we're hoping to see it in renovated grandeur on this summer's trip. (P.S. We did, and it's just as fabulous as before, maintaining its old-world charm.)

For boutique shopping, our own *Marais* area is definitely the place along *rue des Francs Bourgeois* and *rue du Temple*. You can spend all afternoon. My one splurge purchase was a designer winter coat by *Gerard Darel*. Love it!

PASSAGES AND ARCADES

Paris is known for its ancient covered shopping arcades called passages, the same word in both English and French. There is much written on these shopping wonders from ages ago; if you're interested, buy a guide book for the history, specifics, and directions.

The better ones are along *Les Champs Elysées*, inside *Place des Vosges*, and *Palais Royal*. Our all-time favorite, however, is *Galerie Vivienne*. It is one of the most well-preserved with exquisite shopping, including my favorite fabric and scarf shop, *Wolff & Descourtis*, home to the cool designs of *Didier Ludot*. *Très, très cher!!*

Galerie Vivienne

Bernie and I love to take our company to *Galerie Vivienne* for an afternoon outing of classic French ambiance and refreshment at *A Priori Thé* (tearoom), accompanied by a stroll through the unique shops. From old books to great artwork, housewares to designer fashion, great wines to gift items, you can't find a more enjoyable outing, even on a rainy day!

Les Soldes

No chapter on Paris shopping would be complete without a quick mention of the fabulous Paris summer sales or *Les Soldes* during the month of July. It's such a clever game plan to have the biggest, best blow-out for shoppers at the same time each year. If your trip finds you in Paris in late June to late July, watch for the graceful red banners flapping in the breeze on the large department stores, all saying *SOLDES* (Sales). The discount starts out around 10-20% off and goes as high as 70-80% off during the final week. You get to make the choice of great selections at moderately reduced prices or poor selections at really phenomenal prices. Whatever you decide, it's a hoot to jump into this very Parisian experience. Note to avid shoppers—the lines at some of the stores are fierce!

So, this is Linda and Bernie's guide to shopping in Paris. It's not terribly sophisticated or specific, but it *does* give you a common-sense overview. Here are a few more helpful tips.

In ready-to-wear, French sizes tend to run smaller overall because the French are often smaller in stature than Americans. The size ranges are European. For example, I wear a size 7B shoe, but in Paris, I'm a size 38. At home, I wear a size 6 in clothing; in Paris that translates to a 38 or 40 depending on the cut. It's awkward at first, but you'll learn their system. Very politely ask for help if you can find a clerk. There are not check-out counters all throughout the big department stores but rather major paying stations called *les caisses*. Just look for them, and enter the queue. Of course, the smaller boutiques function exactly as our stores do.

Dressing rooms vary from almost none to very nice, depending on the store. It's not unusual to see people trying on articles over their own clothes in front of a mirror right in the aisles of the store. I've also observed that you shouldn't dawdle in the dressing rooms since other shoppers are waiting. Make sure your purchase fits because returning something is an onerous challenge. Bernie and I have spent hours fussing over returns. First, you have to locate the clerk who waited on you, assuming they are working on that particular day. If not, you have to come again and try to find them because they must sign off on the return. Only then can you go to the counter and get your money back. It's one of those complicated processes!

I have made some great purchases in Paris like my designer, cashmere coat. I have also made some pretty bad mistakes (mostly items that ended up being too small), but thankfully none that were terribly expensive. I have worn the heck out of some items and given others to my petite, adult daughter. All the more reason to know what your pocketbook is capable of handling. I've had the best luck with shoe and scarf purchases. Bernie has bought several shirts, a nice linen jacket and also some scarves. And my best purchases always glean compliments from folks at home with the question, "Did you get that in Paris?"

I'll close with a funny story on Bernie. Several years back, his brother took us to the airport in Huntsville. It was not until after we had checked in and were inside the terminal that Bernie turned to me and said, "Damnit, I left my black leather jacket in the back seat of Bill's car. It was my dinner jacket, my only dinner jacket for the whole trip."

"Well," I replied, "looks like we'll be going shopping as soon as we arrive! I'm so sorry, but it's not the end of the world. It's only money!"

Indeed, we soon went to *Au Printemps* in the men's department to look for leather jackets. His selection was moderately priced for Paris at $300. Ugh! Several weeks later, we went to *Le Marché aux Puces*. In the section before the real flea market, there were racks and racks of nice leather jackets for less than half what he had paid. They were probably hot or knock-offs but who would have known or cared? Bernie still bemoans that purchase, and we always laugh out loud when we see black leather jackets anywhere.

Bonne chance (Good luck) as you develop your shopping acumen in Paris.

Purely Paris

For fashionistas, shoes are an issue in Paris because of all the walking. Finally, after eleven years, I've given over to comfort, not fashion—but not without a fight. I've been known to take my gorgeous, fashionable shoes with me in an opaque plastic bag and change before I enter our restaurant of choice! Who cares? Nobody knows me!

For Paris souvenirs and scarves, there is no place as inexpensive as the streets both in and leading up to *Montmartre*, especially if you're looking for small gifts for friends and family back home. No matter where you go with high tourist traffic, you will see the same collection of items—around *Notre Dame*, the Eiffel Tower, the arcades of *Palais Royal* or along *Ile Saint-Louis*. What <u>will</u> be different are the prices. Save your souvenir shopping for a glorious blue-sky day at *Montmartre*.

Our best new discovery in 2013 was a fantastic *epicerie du mond* (world food store) called *Izrael* on *Francois Miron*, one of the Marais' best, family-owned shops. It sells food from five different continents in a quaint, traditional setting—spices, condiments, nuts, olives, olive oil, sardines, dried fruit, nuts, pasta, pickled garlic, capers, and dozens of other hard-to-find delights. *20littlecities.com* referred to it as Ali Baba's cave!

CHAPTER 11

Eating in Paris

Repas à Paris

⌒

In France, cooking is a serious art form and a national sport.

– JULIA CHILD

BERNIE AND I LOVE TO explore the restaurants of Paris, not because we have big appetites or deep pockets, but because we delight in the artistic French presentation of food. Many of our days are built around where we're going to eat! And we are always reading, exploring, and critiquing new restaurants as well as some which are centuries old.

The wave of casualness sweeping the globe has not escaped Paris and is affecting the older celebrated restaurants. The younger, hip crowd appreciates good food but with less fanfare, so new chefs with creative menus and less traditional venues have a fertile ground among the locals. This seems especially true out in the higher *arrondissements* surrounding old Paris. We are fearful that the finesse of style and presentation in fine dining will be lost in this transition just like *le chic* in Parisian fashion. But, as yet, the taste buds certainly are not suffering.

The government of Paris has recently issued a mandate that any establishment calling itself a *restaurant* must serve only naturally prepared food made on the premises. They are trying to preserve what makes Paris so Paris, the culinary specialties of superior quality, unique to the city.

We've already mentioned a few important points about eating, but it won't hurt to reiterate them. Dining is a vital part of French culture, and Parisians eat with gusto. Leaving food on one's plate untouched is a *faux pas* (misstep) and an insult to the chef. Simply stated, the French live to eat because it embodies their *joie de vivre*. It is not only an expression of art, but also a respite for relaxation, a chance to share camaraderie with friends and family, and of course, a chance to sample fine wines. And why then don't French people get fat? The answer is obvious—all the walking and all the steps! And until the last decade, limited exposure to fast food. Sadly, in the past few years, we have seen more and more McDonald's, and our hearts stopped when a Subway opened across the street from our apartment. It had previously been a small mom-and-pop jewelry store. The grand opening of this Subway spilled out into the street with free-flowing champagne, blocking traffic. Only in Paris!

Eating out at every meal is cost-prohibitive for Bernie and me. We always eat our breakfast in the apartment. Then, we either dine out for lunch **or** for dinner, but rarely both in the same day. I have about six meals I can prepare pretty easily in our tiny kitchen. [If you must know, they are spaghetti, salmon with French green beans and Jasmine rice, grilled pork chops with salad, rotisserie chicken and potatoes from the wonderful *boucherie* on *Saint-Antoine,* shrimp scampi over rice, and hamburger steak with salad and fried potatoes.] Once in a while, we also get Chinese take-out. Bernie is such a trouper because he loves anything I prepare.

While in Paris, I consider myself on vacation; cooking is not something that enthralls me. Once I tried to make *bœuf bourguignon*, and it was a total disaster. The meat was tough; the broth was watery; Bernie downed it with effort, and never said a word! I had packed a heavy, oversized French cookbook so as to have the just-right recipe. Duh—I'm not a sophisticated cook at home. For the life of me, I don't know why I thought I could pull it off in Paris!

Continuing our theme for all things six, here are six of our best suggestions for lunch and for dinner along with some special designations. Right away, we'll ask forgiveness. As much as we hate to admit it, we are tourists, *n'est-ce pas?* So, if some of these places seem touristy, oh well. At last check, Trip Advisor had 14,204 entries for places to eat in Paris! The few we are listing have either been stumbled upon or sought out with careful scrutiny in terms of location and price. Some are based on personal recommendations from friends we've met in Paris. They are special to us for a variety of reasons but mainly for the memories we've accumulated over the years.

If you research the top fifty or even the top one hundred restaurants in Paris, only a few of ours will be listed. That is primarily a function of budget. For most of you reading this book, you can certainly find the very expensive places by searching the internet. After you see the prices, you may wonder if there's any place where you can afford to eat. The answer is, "Absolutely!" We're giving you a modicum of mediocrity by Parisian standards, but our list works for us. You can have fun starting your own list via your own memories.

You can Google our suggestions to get exact addresses, phone numbers, and hours of operation. Remember, many places close at least one day a week, and few are open on Sundays. We have used a dollar sign code to express cost—$ being the least expensive ($20-50 per person), and $$$$ ($300-$600 per person) being the most expensive. These price designations include all courses plus wine and are certainly not validated by anything or anyone but our collective memory. So no guarantees, other than hopefully a lovely experience!

BEST PICKS FOR A MEMORABLE LUNCH

1. *Le Moulin de la Galette* (the windmill of the pancake) is your lunch stop going up or coming down from *Montmartre*. This spot actually has a windmill built in 1622 and immortalized in oil by Renoir. (The painting is now at the *Musée d'Orsay*.) When it was turned into a dance hall in the 1860s, it was named for the *"galettes"* (cakes made with flour ground inside the mills) that were sold here. Order the pickled garlic as an appetizer—whole cloves of garlic mixed with large capers which have been marinated in a wonderful brine solution. We much prefer the outdoor dining here if the weather cooperates. **$$**

2. *La Village* is a lovely hide-away near *La Place de Madeleine* tucked on a quaint side passage. After a morning of shopping, it's a restful garden spot, but often quite busy. Try to be seated by noon, even though a little early for Paris. Our best memory here was a ten-year-old devouring steak tartare! $

3. *Musée Jacquemart-André Salon de Thé* is inside the museum of the same name. Before touring the museum, make a reservation for lunch as you enter. If it's a pleasant day, the patio is delightful as well as the classic French tea room. They have delicious quiche, salads, and mouth-watering desserts which you can personally select from a luscious pastry cart. $$

4. *Le Cristal Room* is a divine spot inside the *Baccarat* Museum. After you've drooled over the jewelry and looked through the tiny museum, treat yourself to a very elegant, but pricey lunch with an exceptional presentation. This popular spot for business people offers a tiny terrace, seating four to six. Don't forget your camera; the food is picturesque. $$-$$$

5. *Mariage Frères* gets its name from *Mariage,* the family name of two brothers who started these tea rooms back in the late 1800s. There are locations in Japan, China, and now four in Paris, the newest one on *rue Cler.* The one we like is on an obscure *rue* in the *Marais.* It is a representation of the bygone days of French Indochina. The waiters don white linen suits, and the tea menu is pages long. For dessert, order a *Carré d'or,* translated "a chocolate square in gold leaf." And yes, it has a very thin layer of genuine gold leaf that is edible. *Magnifique*! The tiny restaurant is set amid palm trees and a sun roof, giving the essence of outdoor dining. At the conclusion of your delicious lunch, visit the tea museum upstairs which is historically interesting. $-$$

6. *Le Sergent Recruteur* How surprised we were in 2012 to see that the notorious *Taverne du Sergent Recruteur* had closed. This tavern on *Ile Saint-Louis* was supposedly the place hundreds of years ago where young men were brought to eat, given drink to excess, and

then duped into signing up for the army while intoxicated. (We're not entirely sure this is true, but it made for a good story!) In more recent times, *Le Taverne* was a fun, raucous eatery for large groups, mainly tourists, to come for a one-price meal. The salad was a plate of whole veggies that you cut yourself, followed by a plate of whole sausages, blocks of cheese, a main course, dessert and all the wine you could drink. It was not great food but always a good time. How surprised we were again in 2013 to discover that the restaurant had reopened under the name *Le Sergent Recruteur* with a touch of elegance, a new chef, fine dining, and a few artistic nuances from its past—a suit of armor in the window and artistic renderings inside. The tavern atmosphere had completely vanished, and what remained were chic décor, a remarkable menu, and impeccable service. Their chef came with one Michelin star. The food was the best we had in Paris that year. I had pigeon here for the very first and last time! **$$$**

(Note: Sadly, we found this spot had been shuttered **again** in 2015, supposedly due to financial issues; however, rumors are that it will be back, and so will we!)

BEST PICKS FOR A MEMORABLE SUNDAY LUNCH

1. *L'Hôtel George V* Garden Room is the lifestyle of the rich and famous. Enjoy the beauty of the purple orchids, the chic clientele, and exceptional service. Put on a few airs and act like you belong here! **$$**

2. *La Fermette Marbeuf* is a romantic, renowned restaurant in the 8th district near the *George V* and is perfect after attending Sunday worship services at the American Cathedral of Paris. Ask for the Garden Room and don't take no for an answer. (A reservation made before church will ensure your table.) This back room is a gorgeous example of turn-of-the-century art nouveau and is listed

as a historical monument. Its magnificent glass roof was designed in 1898 by Hubert Martineau. The mural paintings, done in peach and green, bring spring to life and are adorned with a reproduction Botticelli. The story goes that this part of the restaurant was lost for many years and discovered quite by chance. Upon its restoration, the owners had found a true treasure. **$$**

Garden Room at *La Fermette Marbeuf*

Best picks for Sunday brunch

1. *The Tea Caddy* is a tiny British tea room on the Left Bank with outside seating. It's on a little alleyway just past the Shakespeare Bookstore near *L'Eglise Saint-Julien-Le-Pauvre,* the oldest church in Paris. The interior and outer façade are adorned with beautiful wood, and the toilet is five-star! This wonderful nook offers tasty Eggs Benedict and spinach quiche. Don't go too early or the chef will not be on the premises, meaning fewer selections. It's within steps of *Odette Pâtisserie* and the famous cream puffs! **$**

2. *Angelina* on *rue de Rivoli*, one of several locations, was established in 1903. It's quite touristy but fun—long lines, but great *chocolat chaud* on a rainy day. $

Best picks for dinner

1. *Les Ombres* (which translated means "The Shadow or Shade") sits near the Eiffel Tower and offers gorgeous views. The roof is made of steel beams created to mimic the tower and connected with Plexiglas — wherever you are seated, you can see the Eiffel Tower. It's located atop *Musée du Quai Branly*, is quite popular, and requires reservations. $$$

The Plexiglas roof at *Les Ombres,*
showcasing the Eiffel Tower

2. *Le Train Bleu,* right out of the Orient Express, is a classic restaurant located in *Gare de Lyon.* Yes, it's upstairs in a train station, but don't be put off by that! Built in 1900, it owes its celebrity to the forty-one paintings on the walls and ceilings which represent scenes along the old railroad lines. Classic movies, famous former guests, abundant brass, elegant chandeliers, and waxed parquet floors finish off the charm of this special dining experience. Check out the Big Ben bar, the restrooms at the end of the bar, and by all means the pickled garlic served at the bar. If you like steak tartare, the waiters will prepare it at your table. The restaurant was renovated in 2014; all the ambiance remains and with updated restrooms, though I preferred the old ones! **$$-$$$**

Le Train Bleu

3. *Le Grand Colbert* is the location of the movie scene with Diane Keaton and Jack Nicholson in *Something's Gotta Give.* In a good area behind the *Palais Royal,* it's a classic brasserie with traditional French food and

wonderful ambiance. If you like the famous French dessert, *Ile Flottante,* (translated floating island or as Bernie's family says, eggs and snow), you'll find it on the menu here. The arrangement of the restaurant provides quiet nooks for conversation and enjoyment. We had Bernie's seventy-fifth birthday celebration here with family and friends in 2014. (see Chapter 18) And by the way, if you step over the small grillwork on the floor leading to the restrooms, you may still see my lip liner resting there where I accidentally dropped it five years ago! **$$-$$$**

4. *L'ilot Vache,* a corner restaurant on *Ile Saint- Louis,* is all about cows because cows grazed on this land during the sixteenth century. Be sure to read the historical summary about the restaurant on the menu. The table floral arrangements are awesome, and the food is quite tasty, with a one-price menu that is very reasonable. **$$**

5. *Montparnasse 1900* across from the *Montparnasse* train station is a classic brasserie with a one-price menu choice. It's a local favorite. For thirty-three euros at lunch or dinner, your meal includes an aperitif with snack, wine, mineral water, starter, main course, cheese, dessert, and coffee. Who says there are no good deals in Paris? The outdoor area is protected against the weather, though that is where the smokers sit. Watch out for kidneys on the menu here, and know what you're ordering! Step inside for a restroom break because the interior is lovely. **$$**

6. *Bofinger,* the oldest Alsatian restaurant in Paris with classic Alsatian food (sauerkraut, sausages, pork), is just off *La Place de la Bastille.* Insist on sitting downstairs under the stain-glassed dome and expect long lines on Friday and Saturday evenings. It's a local, family favorite. **$$**

FINE DINING (STARRED RESTAURANTS WHERE WE'VE EATEN, THANKS TO FRIENDS AND FAMILY)

If fine dining is one of your must-dos in Paris—and we think it should be at least once—do some homework. Spend a minute with the *Michelin Guide* to better understand what the four-star system means and how the designations are achieved. It's truly a **BIG** deal. We can offer personal comments on these:

1. *Le Pré Catelan* is a three-star restaurant in the huge forest in the middle of Paris, *Le Bois de Boulogne,* along with the ladies of the night! It has a fascinating menu, unbelievable wine list, and unbelievable prices. The highlight of our unusual dinner was a wonderful green apple dessert. When it was delivered to the table, it looked like a shiny, hard, green candy apple; none of us knew how to eat it. The bemused waiters were watching to see our response, and finally one of them suggested that we hit it with our spoons. That was the secret! We gave each apple a good hard whack, and some wonderful deliciousness came oozing out. This meal for four was several thousand dollars! **$$$$**

2. *Le Tour d'Argent* has a very long history, dating back to 1582. Some say this now one-star restaurant is overpriced and has lost its flair, but we found it delightful both times we've eaten here. Duck is the specialty, and when you order it, you are given a souvenir postcard with your authentic duck number. Watching how they carve the duck is worth the expensive dinner. It is also famous for its breathtaking view of *Notre Dame*'s flying buttresses. The wine list is a foot thick (no exaggeration), and the service is impeccable from the moment you enter the door. I loved the fact that the waiters were not snooty, but most gracious and accommodating. Multiple beehives are located on top of the restaurant which add another distinction to this classic Parisian treasure. A funny memory is all the searching we did trying to find the restaurant, which sits on the top floor of a tall building along the river. We looked and looked many times over several years, only to finally discover it just across our most frequented bridge, *Pont Marie.* Our best memory here was celebrating the fiftieth wedding anniversary of Bernie's American cousins. **$$$**

3. *Jules Verne* is a world-famous, one-star restaurant in the Eiffel Tower with stunning views. We have eaten here for lunch on two occasions, never yet for dinner, as dinner reservations must be made a year in advance. This was our first taste of really fine dining. The presentation, especially the desserts, is mind-boggling; this was also our introduction to red champagne or a *Kir Royal. Très bon!* **$$$-$$$$**

4. *Laurent,* a treat from Bernie's French cousins, is a lovely, traditional, one-star restaurant off *l'Avenue des Champs Elysées* with an atmosphere that is quiet and elegant. If you like cheese, their after-dinner cheese cart will amaze and delight your palate. I don't remember the number of different cheeses, but it took quite a while for the waiter to point out the name of each variety. Bernie was in heaven! **$$$**

5. *Benoit* is a one-hundred-year-old bistro which holds the distinction of being the only bistro in Paris with a Michelin star. It is in the *Marais* and within walking distance of our apartment. I read up on the restaurant before going and was forewarned about Americans being seated in the back room. I politely insisted on the lovely front area, and we were seated there with no fuss or bother. The thing I most recall (besides the bill for four, which was $600) was the fantastic *foie gras,* which was served with a puffed pastry-like-bread rather than the usual toast points. It was divine. **$$-$$$**

6. *Le Sergent Recruteur* One-star and already listed **$$$**

CULINARY FAVORITES OF OURS

Just a word or two more about Parisian foods we love, followed by some recipes from our friend, chef, and cooking school host, Charlotte Puckette.

Dessert items seem to top our list and are found on menus at the older, classic eateries where chefs know the recipes. Three of the best are *crème caramel* (flan, Bernie's favorite), *baba au rhum,* and *île flottante* (egg custard with meringue, Linda's favorite). The best *île flottante* is actually a few blocks up from our apartment on *rue Saint-Antoine* at one of the mom-and-pop delicatessens, *Le Sanglier.* It's not available every day, only when the clerk who knows how to make it happens to be working! (And we discovered another great one in 2016 at *Le Coupe-Chou.*)

Some of the best steak tartare is at *Ma Bourgogne* in *La Place des Vosges.* This serving of raw steak is purportedly the largest in Paris—definitely a Bernie, not a Linda, favorite. It can be mixed with many different condiments including capers, salt, pepper, Worcestershire sauce, garlic, onion, mustard, and a raw egg.

Foie gras is offered in many restaurants with varying quality. Goose or duck liver sounds absolutely gross, but it is *très, très bon*. It is served cold as a *paté* or slightly seared. **You can't go to Paris without at least giving it a try.** Save this experience for a really nice restaurant where the quality of *foie gras* will be well above average.

So, we hope you eat your way around Paris as we have. However, I will say that day after day of this rich, high-caloric food will do you in. The remedy is a few days of light *pique-niques* with just fruit, cheese, wine, and bread. And ramp up the walking or the extra calories will definitely hang on!

Purely Paris

Kir Royal is a French cocktail, a variation on a Kir. It consists of *crème de cassis* topped with champagne, rather than the white wine used in a traditional Kir.

Most surprising new information for Linda—According to Bernie, it is cheapest to stand at a bar to eat and drink; it's slightly more expensive to be seated inside; and the most expensive way to enjoy Paris is to sit outside as we love to do. The eating establishment must pay rent to the city for the right to use the sidewalk. Did everyone know this but me?

RECIPES FROM CHARLOTTE PUCKETT[4]

CRÈME ANGLAISE

This velvety pouring custard is the ultimate accompaniment for cakes and tarts and yet, so much more. It is also the velvety sauce for *île flottante*, the decadent touch to a bowl of fruit and the magic of vanilla ice cream.

2 cups (500 g) whole milk
5 egg yolks
1 vanilla pod, split in half lengthwise
½ cup (130 g) sugar

Pour the milk into a small saucepan. Place one half the vanilla bean on a cutting board and using the dull side of the blade, run the knife down the length of the pod to scrape away the seeds. Add the seeds to the milk, wrap the other half of the bean in plastic film and reserve for another recipe. Bring the milk to a boil.

In a medium sized bowl, whisk the yolks and sugar together until light in color and thickened. Remove the milk from the heat and gradually pour into the yolk mixture, whisking constantly. Slowly adding the hot liquid to the egg mixture will temper the yolks so they won't curdle. Continue until all the milk is added. Return the egg/milk mixture to the saucepan and put the pan over medium heat. At this point switch from a whisk to a wooden spoon, stirring constantly using a figure-eight movement to keep the mixture in motion

---

4 Charlotte Puckett: Grand Diplôme graduate of Paris's Le Cordon Bleu, co-author of *The Ethnic Paris Cookbook*, March 2007, as well as a cooking instructor, food consultant, caterer, private chef and hostess. Charlotte says, "Having grown up eating shrimp and grits in my native Charleston, South Carolina, I arrived in Paris—by way of a three-year work stint in Entebbe, Uganda—with limited culinary knowledge, unlimited curiosity and a very big appetite. Curiosity about food has taken me all over Paris and the rest of France in search of new and untried ingredients and products, leading to a solid base from which I have continuously enlarged my knowledge of and appreciation for what goes into the French culinary phenomenon. 'Oh, that looks good—wonder what it is. Maybe I should try it!' has been a constant refrain running through my head for over two decades as I have learned, taught, thought and written about food—and, of course, cooked it."

so it will not stick. Cook until the custard is thick enough to coat the spoon and when you run your finger down the back of the spoon it leaves a clean trace. The custard should reach a temperature of 180° F (80° C), on an instant read thermometer.

Immediately remove the custard from the heat and strain into a 2-quart measuring cup. Refrigerate for at least 4 hours, but the texture and flavor will improve if thoroughly chilled overnight. It will keep in the fridge for several days.

ŒUFS A LA NEIGE/ÎLE FLOTTANTE
(Eggs and Snow or Floating Island)

Meringues
4 egg whites
50 g (3 heaping tablespoons) sugar
Pinch of cream of tartar or salt
2 cups of milk
4 cups of water

Caramel Sauce
1 cup sugar
1/3 cup water
2-3 teaspoons cream
1 tablespoon butter

Crème Anglaise See recipe above
To make the Meringues:

* Spread a clean kitchen towel on a counter near the stove. Combine milk and water and slowly heat until it almost reaches a simmer – 185°F/85°C.
* For the meringues, beat the whites and cream of tartar in the bowl of an electric mixer fitted with the whisk attachment on medium speed

until frothy. Turn the mixer on high speed and add the sugar, spoonful by spoonful. Beat until the egg whites are very stiff and glossy. Do not overbeat.

*   Gently drop spoonfuls of meringue into the simmering water without overcrowding and simmer for 5 minutes on one side, then gently flip and simmer 3 more minutes on the other side. Remove with a slotted spoon and place onto a sheet of baking paper until needed or refrigerate for up to 3 hours.

To make the Caramel Sauce:

Mix the water and sugar in a medium, heavy-bottomed saucepan. Cook over low heat for 5 to 10 minutes. Stir the mixture from time to time by gently swirling the pan. (You do not want to use a spoon as the caramel will stick to it and cause a mess!) Cook until the sugar dissolves and turns a warm chestnut brown. Turn off the heat. Slowly add the cream; this will cause the mixture to bubble up violently so take care to stand back to avoid getting splattered. Once all the cream is in and the bubbling has subsided, add the butter, again, swirling the pan to mix.

To assemble: Pour a ladle of *crème anglaise* into each of six glasses and gently place a meringue in the centre. Dribble the caramel sauce over the top.

CHAPTER 12

Rainy Days

Il pleut!

—⟡—

The rain's very important. That's when Paris smells
its sweetest. It's the damp chestnut trees.

– AUDREY HEPBURN AS SABRINA

SOME PEOPLE LOVE PARIS IN the rain. In fact, they prefer it—claiming doggedly that Paris is more romantic on gray days, brushed in sepia, and dapple-dressed in taupe and brown like a rich part of French history. They insist the rain summons reminiscence and intrigue—an earthiness, ambiance, and bouquet of old Paris. I don't agree, and rainy days are not my favorite. However, Bernie and I have mastered how to constructively spend the rainy days when they come, and come they will. We have learned to persist despite the yucky weather, and we both agree that a rainy day in Paris is far better than a sunny day at home! This chapter will suggest six of our most interesting rainy day outings guaranteed to supplant the dreary dampness.

To clarify—a rainy day to me is one where the rain begins early in the morning and continues all day long. That is quite different from a pop-up rain shower which happens very frequently in Paris. In either case, duck for cover in a little café with an awning, and wait out the rain with a glass of wine or a cup of *chocolat chaud* (hot chocolate), none better than in Paris. (The best we've had is on *Ile Saint-Louis* at *Le Flore en L'Île* overlooking the Left Bank and *Notre Dame.*) One of the clever surprises about Paris is finding heaters and roll-out awnings at most of the sidewalk cafés. The restaurateurs meticulously plan for cool, rainy weather to accommodate their outside clientele.

Bernie and I often disagree over the outside arrangements, however. I get chilly and he doesn't. I don't like the wind blowing my hair, and he rolls his eyes. I want to sit right under a heater turned up full blast, and he gets too hot. So the tap dance between us is often less than good on these rainy day outings. Sometimes, the awnings leak or have cracks in between sections. Ever the gentleman, Bernie volunteers to sit in the cracks and splats and doesn't seem to mind. We even differ on the beverage of choice: wine for him and hot chocolate for *moi.*

Paris is a big, dirty city; rain creates big, dirty puddles which ruin nice shoes. Pack a pair of closed-toe, rainy-day shoes that may be inferior in style but assured to keep your feet dry. To reiterate, always have a raincoat or lightweight poncho (which you can buy on the street) and an umbrella. Ladies **and** gents, this is the day for a very good scarf tucked into your purse or backpack, just in case. Maybe, it's that orange one you packed!

Surely, you're not surprised that we might suggest museums for your rainy day entertainment. Just be very careful to check out each one online. Some are closed on Mondays, and some on Tuesdays, since they are open all weekend. Don't yawn at the word *museum* and equate it with boring. The museums we are recommending are one of a kind. I would venture to say they will be unlike anything you've ever seen before. Pick up a *Where Paris* magazine and seek out different treasures for other rainy days.

(Where Paris is an informative magazine published quarterly in English which showcases all the interesting cultural activities taking place in Paris during the season of publication. Try to find one upon your arrival if you are staying for a while. Copies can be found at the travel information kiosks

located throughout the city or at major hotels. This full-color guide has brought us many wonderful discoveries over the years, and it's free! It lists seasonal events, shops, museums, exhibits, shows, restaurants, and side trips. It's our Bible each year as we explore the newest and chicest about Paris.)

Here are our top six museum picks to cure the rainy day blahs.

Musée Jacquemart-André

Musée Jacquemart-André is on *Boulevard Haussmann.* It was the lovely home of a very well-to-do couple from the 1880s who spent their thirteen-year marriage collecting wonderful art, much of it from Italy. The art collection includes works by Rembrandt, Van Dyke, Botticelli, Bellini, and Carpaccio, to name a few. The home is filled with well-preserved tapestries, sculptures, and frescoes. My favorite feature is a gorgeous, double staircase designed by the architect, Henri Parent, who lost the bid to design the classic Opera House. He vowed that this stairway was his vengeance.

The *Andrés* were steeped in high society and threw huge parties for all of Paris. Their annual income was purported to be the equivalent of €250,000 to €500,000 and this, mind you, was in the late nineteenth century. The *Louvre* at that time encouraged the *Andrés* to purchase the better works of art as the museum did not have the budget. The wife, *Nélie,* decided in 1919 at the death of *Jacquemart* to donate the entire property and its contents to the Institute of France. How lucky for us! The free audio guide is beautifully done and will set the tone of time and place.

As suggested before, stop in for lunch at the tearoom, and sit outside, weather permitting. The patio is fully covered with a large canopy. Bernie and I love this outing. It is so wonderfully French!

Musée Baccarat

Sitting quietly on the tree-lined *Place des Etats-Unis* (Square of the United States) in the 16th *arrondissement* is a small museum that will wow you.

(Before you go in, check out the statue of George Washington and Lafayette in the park.) From the moment you enter, you'll know that a treat awaits. The cascading stairway welcomes you with its red carpet, graced by twinkling, crystal-studded lights. The hand-made, exquisite Baccarat crystal, world renowned, is everywhere—the perfume bottles for Marie Antoinette were made of Baccarat. Walk up the impressive staircase into two huge showrooms displaying gorgeous crystal vases, candlesticks, glassware, chandeliers, and finally exquisite jewelry. Purchase a piece if you can, but I'll warn you that it is all *très, très cher.* Then visit the quaint museum and watch the short but interesting video presentation. Hopefully, you thought to make a luncheon reservation at *Le Cristal Room.* Don't miss the restrooms of mirrored walls alternating with red panels. The sinks are flat and made of sterling silver. Can't find out how to get the water to flow in the sinks? There's a foot pedal underneath! No jeans or shorts here, my friends, and remember that the museum and restaurant are closed on Tuesdays.

Bernie and I have had some great memories at this museum and restaurant, starting with our very first time when we were inappropriately dressed. A movie production crew saved us as they were also in blue jeans. We celebrated a friend's birthday here (the one who introduced us) as a total surprise to her and have dined with other special friends, to no one's disappointment. *Le Cristal Room* is a touch of elegance and a chance to sample quality French food with an excellent presentation for less than a starred restaurant.

Musée Carnavalet

Musée Carnavalet presents the history of the city of Paris. It is free and is certainly the way to spend at least half a rainy day and perhaps longer. It is located in the *Marais* (3rd), right in the heart of the Jewish district. The gardens are worth the trip, even in the rain. It is in two neighboring mansions, *Hôtel Carnavalet* and *Hôtel Le Peletier de Saint-Fargeau.* (The word *hôtel* in French refers to a personal residence of ages ago.) You will learn about the birth of Paris, the French Revolution, and more contemporary displays from famous

Parisian hotels and restaurants which have been shuttered. There are one hundred rooms. Bernie has observed that the tour starts out a little slowly, but be patient—you will love it. And remember that it's closed on Mondays.

Gardens of *Musée Carnavalet*

The Parisians are very proud of this museum and of the fact that it is free to the public. Believe it or not, we found out about it on our first stay in the *Marais* from a stranger on the *Métro*. She was speaking rapid French, but we got the message!

MUSÉE QUAI BRANLY

Mind-boggling is the only word for this museum, which will take an entire day to visit. It traces the history and development of early man through four areas of the world: oceanic islands, Asia, Africa and the Americas. The underlying theme is the preservation of the globe. The entry is along an ascending spiral walkway where a **river** of words is projected on the floor as you are walking, symbolizing the flow of man's language as it moved, developed, and meshed throughout the world. The displays are themselves works of art, many done in leather, and the entire museum is interactive with video kiosks. The gardens outside are untamed and peaceful, full of bamboo and tropical plants. This museum is relatively new and has been a sensation in Paris. Bernie and I found a write-up in *Where Paris* magazine in 2006, the year it opened.

Eat lunch on the very top at *Les Ombres* with the Eiffel Tower in full view. Or come back on a great weather day so the view of the tower will be bright and clear. If you're staying for lunch, no shorts or tennis shoes, and reservations are a must!

MUSÉE NATIONAL DU MOYEN ÂGE OR MUSÉE DE CLUNY

On the Left Bank and perhaps not as well-known, *Musée de Cluny* or Museum of the Middle Ages houses medieval relics, well-preserved Roman ruins, and the overwhelmingly lovely Lady of the Unicorn Tapestries. When I walk into the tapestry showroom, I have to sit down because it takes my breath away. The room is temperature controlled, and the massive hanging tapestries represent the five senses. Each tapestry depicts a lovely maiden with a unicorn involved in some activity that displays either sight, sound, taste, touch, or smell. On our first visit, Bernie admitted that he had never heard of the Unicorn Tapestries. I had, because of a book I had just read of the same name by Tracy Chevalier. It didn't take but a second for him to be overwhelmed and totally impressed. We always have a seat and soak up the majesty of these ancient tapestries.

Lady and the Unicorn Tapestry at *Musée de Cluny*

You will need at least two hours here with a stop in the gift shop to pick out a tapestry replica for your own home. There are plenty of cafés in the area for a cup of *chocolat chaud* or you can have lunch at *Le Procope* where Voltaire and Benjamin Franklin used to dine! Just ask and someone will know the way.

LE LOUVRE

I have already mentioned the wonders of *Le Louvre* in the chapter on strolling, but with a focus on the gardens. The museum itself is a great adventure for a rainy day. First of all is the structure itself: a massive, magnificent royal palace. Also the large galleries of sculptures, the downstairs remnants of the original palace wall, the Napoleonic apartments, and the relics of the ancient Middle Eastern cultures—all are superb! It's a trip around the world in one spot and simply **not to be missed**. Yes, without question, it is overwhelming; that's why you need an entire day if you have the luxury. I've been at least six or seven times and still can't find my way around, but each time, I am awed by something new. Study up before you go, or pay a guide to help you out.

Take Line 1 to the *Palais Royal/Musée du Louvre* subway stop. Enter from below through the *Carrousel du Louvre* shopping center. If you don't have tickets, there is a *TABAC* store near the queue which sells the tickets at the same price as inside, but with almost no wait. If the security queue is really, really long, find the escalators up and out; there is an alternate entry site that is little-known. Ask a local and they will help you find it. Thanks to Bernie for all this secret info!

Once inside, spend a minute looking over the detailed English guide to find the items you most want to see. People literally run for the *Mona Lisa*, *Venus de Milo* and *Winged Victory*. If these are musts for you, by all means, seek them out. If not, just meander and take the day to see as much as you can. We guarantee that you will get lost, but what's the hurry? It's pouring rain outside.

For lunch, take a break, go up the escalator in the main entry hall to the outside. Look across the palace grounds to find *Café Marly*. If you want to sit outside on the covered terrace, make a reservation. While you're eating your club sandwich or smoked salmon, you'll be looking out across the pyramid and reflecting pools of the fabulous palace. For three consecutive years here, we had the same waiter, Sebastian, and were so sad to discover that he had left to start his own restaurant. We've never been able to link up with him again, but perhaps one of these days, he'll pop up when we least expect it!

I realize that museums are not for everyone. Many think they're more a chick thing, but I must say that Bernie enjoys our museum outings as much as I do. Gals, if your men are rebelling, send them off to the Army Museum at *Les Invalides* where Napoleon is buried. They can get lost in war minutia for three or four hours while you get lost in the *Louvre*. Just have a rendezvous point that you both can find.

Here's to short-lived rain and many fun explorations.

Purely *Paris*

"*Tournez à gauche*" means to the left; "*tournez à droite*" means to the right; and "*Tout droit*" means to go straight ahead.

CHAPTER 13

Summer Days

C'est l'été

—

I love Paris in the summer, when it sizzles.

– COLE PORTER

MAYBE BECAUSE I'M A SOUTHERN gal from Alabama, I am definitely more at home in Paris on beautiful, sun-splashed days. There's something remarkable about Parisian architecture etched against a vibrant blue sky, the ripple of warm breezes, and the ease of care-free clothing that release the best in me. There's no umbrella to fight or jacket to tire of holding, no puddles to jump, or traffic spray to avoid. It's just my two feet in cool easy shoes, the excitement of the city, the great people-watching, the buzz of conversation, the clang of traffic, the blaring of horns, and the surprises that are beckoning. When the sun comes out, so do the Parisians. I relish in it!

Paris in the summer sun is a smorgasbord of potential! It was extremely difficult to select only six of our favorite summertime outings. Some are date-specific, which means, of course, that your trip has to coincide exactly. The others can be done anytime the weather is nice. And absolutely, don't forget the opportunity to do one of our strolls or discover a new one on your own! Or visit the lovely *Musée Rodin* which is mostly an outdoor, sunny-day experience in the gardens.

La Fête de la Musique (June 21)

June 21 is the Summer Solstice—the official start to summer and the longest day of the year. Parisians celebrate with a citywide festival of music. It stays light until ten o'clock, so the celebrating goes on and on! Around every corner, church, and park is a host of musical opportunities. This event is coordinated by the city of Paris, and an official program by *arrondissement* is printed each year in magazine fashion and distributed in the subway stations and local newspapers. No matter where you might be staying in Paris, there will be something to participate in, or you can easily subway-hop to different *arrondissements* to select what suits your tastes. One of the best locations is around *La Place des Vosges.* Each section of the old arcade hosts a different local group—jazz, vocal, rock, folk, even classical. And if classical music is your preference, the Paris symphony plays at the *Louvre* around nine o'clock. The concert is free, and you can sit on the floor under the glass pyramid! Good luck on getting inside, however. The queue starts about five thirty and winds around the grounds. We tried one year but waited much too late to get inside.

Bernie and I often plan our trip around *La Fête de la Musique* because we love everything about it.

Bastille Day Parade and Fireworks *Quatorze Juillet* (July 14)

July 14 is the French Fourth of July, the anniversary of the French Republic, and the overthrow of the monarchy. Please don't forget that Paris is Bernie's hometown; naturally, he is always thrilled to experience this national *fête.* The day is broken into two parts: the parade in the morning and the fireworks at night.

Televised live and attended by more folks than *Le Tour de France,* the parade is a meticulously planned event. It's held along *l'Avenue des Champs Elysées.* If you want to participate, go very early and stake out your spot, which unfortunately means you will have to stand for several hours. It begins mid-morning with a flyby, very loud and **very** impressive. The fighter jets release exhaust streamers of *bleu, blanc et rouge* (blue, white and red), the colors of the French flag. The presiding French president is always the grand marshal. The parade line-up is France's elite, including police, firemen, *La Garde Republicaine* (police on horseback), all the armed services, and flyby's of every example of aircraft, weaponry, and artillery. *Les Pompiers de Paris* or the firemen draw the biggest round of applause. After the parade, we suggest you leave in a hurry and find a spot for lunch because the subways will be packed like sardines. You will be crushed, jammed, stepped on, and suffocated from the lack of air conditioning.

Bastille Day flyby, the start of the festivities on July 14

At our first parade, we stood in almost the exact spot where Bernie had stood with his mother when he was a little boy of seven or eight, and it was very emotional for him. A flood of memories brought tears to his eyes, and the thrill of being able to recreate his childhood at this late age was awesome. I was wide-eyed with curiosity, trying to process all the new visuals, the sounds, the crowd, and of course, Bernie's raw emotion.

The fireworks in the evening are staged at the Eiffel Tower. If your trip is going to include July 14th, reserve a fireworks-watching space at least six months ahead of time because the venues fill up very quickly. We have done several different things—dinner cruises on the *Seine*, a special meal in a restaurant atop the *Montparnasse* Tower (*Le Ciel de Paris*) where we were up above the fireworks, and once a jaunt to the Eiffel Tower on our own. I don't recommend the latter as it's hard to find a good viewing spot, and the crush of humanity afterwards is overwhelming. If you choose this last adventure, take a dinner and the provisions to sit on the ground.

Bastille Day fireworks from the Eiffel Tower

Here's what happened on our one independent outing. We were eager to get to the Eiffel Tower via subway but soon noticed an on-rush of people as we exited. Our enthusiasm waned quickly because we didn't have a well-thought-out plan. In fact, we didn't have a plan at all! We walked and walked and walked, up one street and down another, fighting the crowds.

"Gee, Bernie. Look around us—everyone has a picnic, and we have nothing. We didn't even bring anything to sit on," I said with frustration.

"Yeah, where do you think we should go?" Bernie asked with his usual dependence on my input.

"You're asking me? I have no idea. I don't have a clue where we are, where the fireworks will appear in the sky—I've never been here before, remember?" I said with agitation.

Then pointing across an open area, Bernie said, "Those folks over there look nice. Let's go sit on the ground next to them."

And we did. They were amicable—some French, some American—and they even shared their champagne. Then we waited. . . and waited. . . and waited for it to get completely dark, which was close to eleven o'clock—over three hours! Suddenly, we started hearing the fireworks but could see **absolutely** nothing.

"Good Lord!" I whined, "We've waited all this time, and we can't see anything! I am **so** disappointed!"

Bernie agreed, but we laughed with our new-found friends who didn't seem to mind that the fireworks weren't visible. All was good until we started trying to leave. It was madness and one of the few times I've been scared in Paris. Mobs of people moved like waves trying to enter the subway station, and I feared getting trampled. The crowd, pushing and shoving, was in total control of us. Our advice on this particular night is to avoid the subways until you get well away from the Eiffel Tower area. Just walk slowly home!

In the last several years, we've noticed that many people sit on the bridges, so that may be our next vantage point. (If you're a real coward, you can stay in your apartment or hotel room and watch all the activity on television. Please, no!) The fireworks are *très magnifique,* gracefully set to classical music, and meant to be experienced in person. Make a good plan for an unforgettable *soirée* (evening outing). You will not be disappointed however you view *le feu d'artifice* (the fireworks).

PIQUE-NIQUES

Give us a blue sky, eighty degrees, an appetite, and we're off to one of our best summer day outings, the *pique-nique*. Our first stop is at our favorite *boulangerie* for sandwiches. We also take cheese, a bottle of wine for Bernie, a bottle of water for me, and some squares of *chocolat*.

Paris is full of green spaces, tiny obscure parks that are not overrun with people. There are several within easy walking distance of our apartment. Or we find a spot along the river which is dotted with benches. Of course, I have to fuss a little over this and make it a project. I take paper towels, some big cloth napkins to serve as lap trays, and a towel to sit on. Bernie could care less, but he lets me do my thing. He takes a Sudoku book, and I take a crossword puzzle for afterward. We might just relax for two hours after we eat and take in the solitude and people-watching. Bernie sneaks a nap. What a wonderful lazy, summer outing!

PARCS

The major parks in Paris are easily identified because most are enclosed in stately twelve-foot, wrought-iron fencing. Each spire or spike has a gold-leaf *fleur-de-lis* on top which requires meticulous care. This adds a majestic touch and an unmistakable boundary. Parisians flock to their major parks for lunch, for a jog, for wedding photos, or to allow their children to frolic and play. Families love the *parcs* for Sunday outings and strolls.

Le Jardin du Luxembourg is probably our favorite. It is on the Left Bank, is massive with fifty-five acres, and trumpets an elegance that surpasses the others. In this one park, you will find the gorgeous Senate building for the state of France; a *Medici* fountain with Poseidon on top of a waterfall, flowing into a shaded wading pool (gorgeous spot for a picnic); a gigantic lake where youngsters rent wooden boats to sail by pushing them around the edge with big sticks (just as Bernie did as a boy); palm trees; ancient statues; beehives; and a quaint, but very worthy art museum. I didn't mention the food stands, the ponies to ride, and a very good restroom. It's fifty cents but clean and worth it!

Parc Monceau, one of the oldest parks in Paris, is located in the 8th *arrondissement* in a high-rent, residential area. It is a more compact park and not as many acres as *Le Luxembourg,* but it has more hideaway nooks, and a circular walkway around the perimeter lined with green benches, instead of the familiar green chairs. We usually don't have a problem securing a bench for our picnic lunch. Joggers pound the small lane of pavement during the lunch hour while businessmen in their suits eat ham sandwiches. The park has a huge playground for the kiddies and gigantic older trees, guaranteeing plenty of shade on a hot day. One frequent sight are the nannies from upscale homes pushing young tots under their charge. It's very much a stroller brigade! There is also a fairly good restroom at the main entrance for a nominal fee.

We've shared only two of our favorite parks. Others we've visited include: *Parc des Buttes-Chaumont, Jardin des Plantes* (Paris's Botanical Garden), *Bois de Boulogne, Bois de Vincennes, Parc de Bercy,* and *Parc de la Villette.* All are lovely with distinguishing features. If none of these are close to where you are staying, don't dismay. Stroll around your area, and I'm quite sure you will run across a park right under your nose.

PÈRE LACHAISE CEMETERY

At the risk of sounding macabre, I am recommending a summer day outing to Paris's largest cemetery, covering one hundred and ten acres. It opened in 1806, and all through the years has been rumored to be haunted. Unlike most American cemeteries, save those in New Orleans, Parisian burial plots are all above ground, elaborate, and exquisitely sculpted. None are more beautiful than those at *Père Lachaise.* You can spend a long afternoon meandering and looking for the graves of the famous—Molière, Chopin, Picasso, and the most visited, Oscar Wilde, to name a few. Wilde's tombstone is covered with lipstick from female admirers kissing the marker. If you saw the movie "Phantom of the Opera," *Père Lachaise* was the setting for the cemetery scene.

It is still a functioning cemetery today, accepting new burials; however, there are certain qualifications for entry, and the waiting list is long. Many of the burial plots are passed from generation to generation.

Wear comfortable shoes as the walking is arduous with winding paths, exposed tree roots, and broken patches of sidewalk. Don't do as we did and take a picnic lunch!

"Bernie, why is everyone looking at us so funny? Do you suppose we shouldn't be having a picnic?" I asked, after spreading out our lunch on one of the benches.

"Well, I don't know," Bernie said. "I think you're making too much of it, but maybe we **have** committed a *faux pas*! I'm hungry, so let's just eat and leave. We won't linger."

"I don't think we should talk very much either. People are very quiet here, and I'm so wishing we hadn't done this. Too late now! Who knew we were making such a mistake!"

Meaning no disrespect, we finished our picnic lunch amid plenty of derisive looks from passersby. We threw our trash away quickly and continued on our way.

We thoroughly enjoyed the quiet beauty, the carvings, the inscriptions, the history lessons. I'm glad we went, and we should probably return without a picnic lunch!

MONTMARTRE

"Bernie, I think it's a *Montmartre* day!" I squeal, after looking out our apartment window to blue skies. "Hurry! Let's get dressed and go eat lunch at *Chez Plumeau*. Then, I'd like to walk down the backside of the mountain where we saw the wine festival parade. Remember?"

"Sure, sounds good to me," says the ever-agreeable Bernie. "It'll be crowded because the weather's so nice, but maybe we can find some out-of-the-way spots and then have a late afternoon aperitif at *La Maison Rose*."

"Ah, yes, my perfect Paris day!" I croon.

"Silly girl! How many times can you go to *Montmartre* in one lifetime?" Bernie says with a twinkle in his eye.

If I had only one day to visit Paris, I would spend it at *Montmartre*. It represents the best of old Paris to me in one giant array of authenticity, history,

Sacré Cœur atop *Montmartre*

and charm. It's what I've always imagined Paris to be. The narrow, barely passable *rues* weave up and down the mountain from all sides, amid hundreds and hundreds of steps, broken wine bottles, and litter. As strange as that may sound, it fits together in a tapestry that suits my eye and my heart. These are the streets of Renoir, Degas and young *avant garde* artists like Picasso, Van Gogh, and Toulouse-Lautrec—streets so narrow that today's city buses and delivery trucks are specially downsized to traverse the tight corners.

Originally, *Montmartre* was a rural village made up of windmills and vineyards and working class peasants. It transitioned into the Bohemian district with every kind of artist rubbing elbows with raucous public entertainment—dance halls, cabarets, prostitution. It represented sexual freedom and revolutionary politics. The streets of *Montmartre* seem to whisper their history, their secrets, and their nostalgia to me. I have a definite kinship with the area which is hard to describe.

Our entry point is via the *Métro* station called *Abbesses* which positions visitors about half-way up the mountain. (Or, if you wish, you can start at the very bottom of the mountain with a quick glance at *Le Moulin Rouge* and the red light district of *Place Pigalle.*) The *Abbesses* station exit is picture-worthy because it is one of the few remaining examples of art nouveau. It spills out into the beautiful *Square Jehan Rictus.* The *Mur des Je t'aime* –Wall of Love—is an unusual mural in the small square. Take a minute to look at the "I love you" phrases in every language imaginable. Just down the street is a funicular for those who aren't able to do all the steps. But if you're able, walking up will be memorable. Once on our walk up, we got caught in the middle of a movie scene. Fabulous!

What makes *Montmartre* so special? There are old cafés; characteristic posts which line the streets (and now keep cars from parking on the sidewalks); window boxes bulging with red geraniums; art galleries; souvenir shops; a few good restaurants and many mediocre ones; a tram; vineyards; a couple of great museums; exquisite views off both sides of the mountain; original art work at *La Place du Tertre;* and the crown jewel, *Le Sacré Cœur*—a majestic white basilica that bursts from the mountain top like a vanilla ice cream cone. If you're lucky, there's even an organ grinder belting out French songs in the main square. If you only go up to see the *Sacré Coeur,* you will have missed the heart and soul of the area. Plan large because *Montmartre* is an all-day outing with miles of walking and hours of discovering. It is one of the most romantic stages in Paris, all the more reason to relish it with your lover beside you. For Bernie and me, sharing this dot of real estate is as good as Paris has to offer us on a summer day.

If you're hesitant to walk through *Montmartre* on your own, set up a tour with a Parisian friend of ours, Ann Jeanne, a native of Paris. Google her at *www.afriendinparis.com.* Through her eyes, you'll discover a special slice of Paris life, made even more enjoyable because of her fluent English spoken with a charming French accent. Ann is personal, chic, and knows the unusual spots of Paris that you won't find in the travel guides. Her tours are individualized, done at your own pace, and will be one of your best Paris memories!

At the end of your summer day outing, conclude hand-in-hand by capturing a sunset on your favorite bridge somewhere along the river between nine and ten o'clock. Breathe in the smell of the city. Walk slowly home as the evening blanket of beauty quiets your spirit for a gentle night's rest.

Purely Paris

If you're in the market for original artwork, *Montmartre* is the best spot, but be aware that many of the local artists do not accept a credit card. Be prepared with cash or run down the mountain to an ATM as we had to do!

The absolute worst thing about Paris in August is the heat without air conditioning. In 2013, we lived through 96° F. and in 2015, survived three 100° days. The only really cool spot was the *Monoprix* meat market.

CHAPTER 14

Summer or Autumn?

L'Eté ou l'automne?

In Heaven, it is always autumn.

– JOHN DONNE

IT WAS DECIDED WELL IN advance. For our tenth journey to Paris in 2014, we would go in mid-September for two months to coincide with Bernie's seventy-fifth November birthday. Previously, we had only experienced Paris in late spring or summer. A seventy-fifth birthday is a milestone, and as Bernie was prone to say, "Who knows what the future will bring? I want to spend my 75th in Paris!"

What started out as a casual conversation about having a low-key birthday celebration gained momentum with each passing day. It erupted and expanded into a mega merriment of company, parties, and receptions with so much food we almost exploded. Family was invited— some came; some did not. But the guests who did had a communal blast. The energy we exerted was Herculean, netting a pleasing but thorough fatigue by the end of each day. To say we came home exhausted from the trip was an understatement, but we had no regrets at having done it the way we had. Read more about the birthday bash in the next chapter.

As you might think, we had expectations and assumptions about what Paris would be like in the fall of the year. How were the sunsets, the crowds, the fashion, the food, the markets, the weather? We got answers to all of our questions—some we liked, and some we definitely didn't. The conclusion was just as I had expected: we much prefer Paris in the summer, but we found new adventures to expand our cultural understanding of Paris in a different season. Now we must go at Christmas!

Preparing and packing for the trip were much more cumbersome for me with boots, bulky sweaters, coats, heavier scarves, gloves, hats—more weight meant ultimately fewer clothes and cleverer coordination. I was sick to death of certain outfits by the time I got home. Summer is definitely easier, lighter, and freer for us females. The guys hardly tell the difference. Ugh!

The weather was our biggest plus—which was just pure luck. July and August had been cool and rainy that year in Paris, so mid-September and all through October were like a pleasant, belated summertime. It was never hot, but oh so pleasant, with lovely days of sunshine, gentle breezes, and gorgeous, autumn blue skies. Not until the last ten days did we get a taste of the cold, gray pall which can hover over Paris. Even that was lovely against the river and bare trees. Coats, boots, scarves, and gloves that had sat dormant in the closet for the early weeks suddenly were with us on every outing. It was during that period where we stayed in a different apartment to give ours over to company coming in for the birthday bash. Unfortunately, the coldest stint we had coincided with the greatest amount of walking. Our different apartment off *Boulevard Beaumarchais,* though lovely on the inside, was remote and inconvenient, compared to our usual circulation near *rue Saint-Paul.* We went from everything at our fingertips to walking a half mile just to get a morning baguette!

I hated the shorter days. Just as in America, by mid to late October, it was dark by five o'clock (the time change from daylight savings coming a week ahead of the States). No more after-dinner walking for two miles to watch the sun play on the *Seine* or to capture a gorgeous sunset at nine-thirty. It was hard to eat stylishly late when it got dark so early; we broke with Parisian tradition and found seating before seven o'clock, generally impossible in Paris. People were still out and about, but the ambiance was totally uninteresting *sans* the daylight—a bit like flat champagne. I disliked it more than Bernie, which was predictable.

One special autumn delight happened in October when we were present to see the Eiffel Tower turn pink for Breast Cancer Awareness month. In typical French fashion, the superb light show was accompanied by classical music.

The Eiffel Tower turns pink for Breast Cancer Awareness

I found out about this on Twitter, and we just happened to be at the exact right spot to watch the Tower go completely dark and then slowly come back to life, layer by layer, in bright neon pink!

Bernie took the dark, short days and made them into a positive, which is partly why he's such a neat guy. He loved having the chance to take night photographs of special landmarks with his super sophisticated camera—which he did, *ad infinitum*. In the summertime, we're ready to call it a day by ten o'clock just as it's getting fully dark. Unless we stay out until midnight, there's never a chance to take night photos. Bernie learned a great deal and loved experimenting with the different stops, speeds, and lenses; plus, he had a great teacher in one of our visitors. Thank you, Charles!

The food was surprisingly different in the fall, much heavier. Instead of light, delicious salads and starters, restaurants were serving heavy soups, stews, and root veggies—a function of what was available at the markets. Surprisingly the markets were open for their usual hours, and people shopped profusely for apples, pears, chestnuts, figs, mushrooms, pomegranates, and items I couldn't identify. My favorite—the cherries—were nowhere to be seen, a summer-only phenomenon. But we did enjoy several rounds of roasted chestnuts from street corner vendors.

The absolute biggest surprise of this trip was the lack of autumn color in the foliage. Save for a clinging, ivy-like plant growing on certain buildings called *vigne vierge* (somewhat like our Virginia creeper), there was only a hint of yellow, no red or orange. Who knew there were no maple trees? Mostly the leaves turned brown and fell off. Even on our late October river cruise down the Rhine, there was no color, contradicting all of those television ads for Viking!

The autumn leaves at *Montmartre*

Bernie's cousin, Laurie, attributed some of the lack of color to the very, very wet summer. Ignorance ruled here as I failed to do any research and expected Paris to be alive with fall color. What a big negative for me!

The fall fashion was lovely as expected, and the store windows were replete with scrumptious coats, sweaters, tailored winter suits, boots, and dazzling winter scarves. All of this contributed to a more noticeable sense of chic than we've witnessed in recent summer jaunts, where high fashion seemed to have lost its grip on Paris. Christmas decorations, Christmas lights, and Christmas windows began to appear during the final days of our visit in November, and the shoppers were flooding the streets in holiday anticipation. We delighted in the windows at *Au Printemps*.

The idea of fewer people overall was another mistaken concept. It was just as crowded to me as in the summer. Bernie disagreed, but I found all the favorite tourist spots to be as jammed as ever. At *Notre Dame* and along *Les Champs*, it might as well have been July. Perhaps there were fewer teenagers, but the large tour groups from all over the world more than made up for them.

In late September, we found ourselves right in the middle of Fashion Week! I was ecstatic; Bernie, non-pulsed. I said to him, "Get your butt up and let's go take some pictures of this. We may never have this chance again!"

Fall Fashion week…*Oh là là*

And so we did. With a little help from the internet, I was able to pinpoint where the major designer fashion shows were being held. Of course, we had no credentials or tickets, and without special privileges, all we could do was stand outside and ogle. And ogle we did! Bernie performed with great finesse as a new member of the *paparazzi*. One model even stopped for him, posed, and waited until he took the shot! That cranked his tractor, as we say in the South. I thought the entire experience was just a hoot, but a little went a long way. After a week, we were maxed out but had some fun photos to share on our blog.

Whatever time you go to Paris will be better than any time spent at home. However, consider what you like and don't like about my seasonal comparisons and select the time that best suits your personality. With a little imagination, Paris will be enthralling whenever you go!

CHAPTER 15

Happy Birthday, Bernie!

Bon anniversaire, Bernard!

Everything ends this way in France - everything. Weddings,
christenings, duels, burials, swindlings, diplomatic affairs
(birthdays) - everything is a pretext for a good dinner.

– JEAN ANOUILH

THIS BOOK WOULD NOT BE complete without a few paragraphs on Bernie's
birthday bash.

Take a minute and reread some of my introduction describing Bernie's
life journey. He was whisked away from Paris at age ten and vowed as a
middle-aged man to spend as much time as he could back in his native city
with his remaining original family. His only birthday request of me was to
spend his seventy-fifth in Paris. How could I refuse? I knew that I would
not like autumn; I knew I would hate the short days and cold weather; I
knew I would struggle with packing heavier clothes; and most of all, I knew
I would miss the delicious cherries which are such a part of my Paris summer. But I said not a word, gritted my teeth, and we were off with a smile
for our fall escapade.

The birthday guests were two sets of cousins—one from America, one
from Soultz, France— along with Bernie's son and significant other from

Nashville, Tennessee. The first birthday event was a cooking class for six of us with our friend, Charlotte Puckett. (We knew about this class from her partner and our friend, Richard Nahem of *www.eyepreferparis.com*. You can book the cooking class directly from this web site.) Charlotte's apartment was just off famous *rue Cler*, a pedestrian street near the Eiffel Tower. Her apartment itself was worth the outing. The entrance opened into a well-equipped and very large kitchen (unusual for Paris) with a spacious table for food prep and eating. The rest of the apartment was accessible by a spiral staircase.

There was basically one room per floor—first a living room, then a bedroom and bath, then an attic area for her children. Fabulous, and oh, so Parisian. Would I want to handle this arrangement every day of my life? No, but for us it was enthralling and right out of a story book.

After a crisp, cool walk through a local market and bakery with Richard, we started our cooking class with hot chocolate and wonderful apple turnovers, then got right to work. Our menu consisted of three courses:

First course: Seared sea scallops with orange-ginger sauce and caramelized fennel

Second course: Roasted duck breast with fig *gastrique* (sauce with port, shallot, rosemary, figs, and raspberries) and oven-roasted fingerling potatoes with coarse salt

Third course: Chocolate *fondant* (flourless chocolate cake) with *crème Anglaise*

Everyone helped with preparation; then we ate the fruit of our labor until we were stuffed. I learned the correct way to separate an egg yolk from the white. As my mother had taught me, I cracked the egg and tried to separate the yolk by gently tossing it from one half of the shell to the other.

"No, no!" called Charlotte, "Just put the whole egg gently in your hand and let the white drain between your fingers into a bowl."

Who knew I had been doing it wrong all these years? Diane, Bernie's cousin, learned how to cut a piece of parchment paper in the shape of a circle for the *fondant* pan. She was thrilled and thought the entire cooking class was worth the investment just for that little jewel of new information. We laughed and dined amid too many glasses of wine, and crafted a marvelous memory.

Cooking school with Linda and Bernie's cousin, Diane

The second big birthday bash was a luncheon hosted by Bernie's American cousins at the hottest new hotel in Paris, the *Peninsula* on *avenue Kléber*. The top floor restaurant is called *L'Oiseau Blanc* (The White Bird), and its theme is centered on a missing plane by the same name from the Lindbergh era. Replicas of the plane and its engine sit in the restaurant with views from the roof top that are as good as the food. We had a delicious lunch for eight with a birthday dessert for Bernie consisting of a yummy pistachio ice cream, fruit, cookie bites and *chantilly* or whipped cream.

A replica of *L'Oiseau Blanc, the White Bird*

Bernie with dessert at L'Oiseau Blanc

Here's an interesting side note: The bar of this hotel (once a government building) is where Henry Kissinger signed the peace accord with Vietnam to end the war. Wow! It's Paris, and there's history in the most unexpected places.

The third birthday event, a cocktail party, confirmed that Paris has become our second home. Our ever-widening circle of friends and neighbors were invited along with family, including our landlady, her husband, and her son who came bearing the gift of a *Hermes* tie for Bernie! Our friend, Richard, volunteered to host the party at his apartment, which is just sixty seconds from ours. Of course, our caterer was Charlotte Puckette, who did some divine *hors d'oeuvres* for the occasion, the most exceptional of which were chicken kabobs in a wonderful peanut butter sauce. The French love peanuts, but rarely do you see peanut butter in the grocery aisles. However, everyone raved about the sauce which I thought was hilarious. Perhaps they didn't know what was in it. (Charlotte, mind you, is from South Carolina, so she is no stranger to peanut butter!)

It is hard to convey what this festive evening meant to Bernie. He was two feet off the floor that night as he had the love of his present life (*moi*), his dear son, his favorite cousins, new friends and neighbors—all in a very personal setting in his hometown. I can't begin to describe the gleam in his eye or the tenderness in his persona. It was only half of my birthday gift to him. I had to pull him back down to Earth to get back to our apartment, and even though it was cold and gloomy outside, his heart was overflowing with copious pleasure and maybe a little too much champagne!

The other half of my birthday gift happened two nights later. We had the official birthday dinner for just family at *Le Grand Colbert*, a classic French restaurant near *Palais Royal*. If you recall, it was the scene of one of the memorable episodes from the movie *Something's Gotta Give*. The restaurant is bedecked with brass fixtures and laden with palm trees, ceiling fans, and ambient lighting so that it truly does emanate a nostalgic link to the past. What a perfect setting, a great welcome, a special menu with Bernie's name on it, good service, and good food. It is not a starred restaurant, but the best my pocketbook could handle for eight people! The memory will remain forever, especially for Bernie and me. We've had better food; we've had better service; we've had more dramatic settings. But the warm glow surrounding our party and the clamor of happy conversation will never be as sweet.

"Happy 75th, Bernie. Here's to you and your Paris!"

CHAPTER 16

Miscellaneous Delights

Méli-Mélo

~~~⟡~~~

**Though I often looked for one, I finally had to
admit that there could be no cure for Paris.**

– PAULA McCLAIN, *THE PARIS WIFE*

THIS HAS BEEN THE HARDEST chapter to write. It was supposed to be a chapter devoted to our favorite memories, locations, and outings. Neither Bernie nor I could produce a small enough list. After many twists and turns, it's ended up being simply a little of this and a little of that, or as the French would say *méli-mélo*. Some things are too special to omit from our book, and this chapter is the catch-all of good "stuff" that we love which has not been previously emphasized. There is a store façade on *rue Saint-Paul* called *Méli-Mélo* which we walk past every day, and thus the inspiration for the chapter title.

Before I begin, I fear all the superlatives about Paris may have begun to run together. Like the little boy who cried wolf, we may have numbed you with too many descriptive adjectives and adverbs! That is understandable, of course, **until** you actually come to Paris and realize, as the opening quote says, that there is no cure. Then you will understand just how difficult it is to capture Paris in any way other than superlatives, and you will also appreciate how hard it is to select your favorites.

Our travel story would not be complete without more on *La Place des Vosges*. This ancient residential community, arcade, and park[5] is minutes from our apartment. The history is included in the footnote, and I hope you will read it. Today, the park is bordered with trees on all sides, which was not always the case; their introduction was quite controversial. Though lovely, they are a big lure for birds, and you know the end result! Still it's a fabulous mecca for families, lovers, and children. It is strikingly beautiful due to the uniform building facades surrounding the green space. The arcade is home to excellent art galleries and a three-starred restaurant, *L'Ambroisie*. It is some of the pricier real estate in Paris. Don't miss an evening stroll through this lovely spot.

A *Hermes* scarf in Paris costs about €500 or $650. When Bernie's French cousins, Pierre and Laurie Verdier, were visiting several years ago, we were in one of the *haute couture* shopping areas off *Les Champs, Avenue Montaigne*. Laurie took us inside the *Hermes* shop under the convincing pretense of shopping for a friend of hers, asking me if I thought her friend would like this scarf or that

---

5 Originally known as the *Place Royale*, the *Place des Vosges* was built by Henri IV from 1605 to 1612. A true square (140 m × 140 m), it embodied the first European program of royal city planning. It was built on the site of the *Hôtel des Tournelles* and its gardens: At a tournament at the Tournelles, a royal residence, Henri II was wounded and died. Catherine de Medicis had the Gothic complex demolished, and she removed to the Louvre Palace.

The *Place des Vosges*, inaugurated in 1612 with a grand *carrousel* to celebrate the wedding of Louis XIII and Anne of Austria, is the prototype of all the residential squares of European cities that were to come. What was new about the *Place Royale* in 1612 was that the housefronts were all built to the same design, probably by Baptiste du Cerceau,[1] of red brick with strips of stone quoins over vaulted arcades that stand on square pillars. The steeply-pitched blue slate roofs are pierced with discreet small-paned dormers above the pedimented dormers that stand upon the cornices. Only the north range was built with the vaulted ceilings that the "galleries" were meant to have. Two pavilions that rise higher than the unified roofline of the square center the north and south faces and offer access to the square through triple arches. Though they are designated the Pavilion of the King and of the Queen, no royal personage has ever lived in the aristocratic square. The *Place des Vosges* initiated subsequent developments of Paris that created a suitable urban background for the French aristocracy.-Wikipedia

one. Suddenly, she was buying the one that I really loved and then brought it over to me, saying that it was actually a surprise gift for me. I was shocked beyond words at her clever and very touching gesture since I was a newcomer in the family circle. I will never forget her thoughtfulness, and it was the genesis of a tender friendship which we have cultivated through the years. And on our tenth autumn trip, she did it again—a beautiful cashmere winter scarf— bright orange, with matching gloves. What fun and so thoughtful!

We've already referenced *La Place du Tertre,* the famous art square, sitting atop *Montmartre.* If the weather is pleasant, the local artists abound, creating and selling their paintings. One day, we spotted a striking painting of a classic French mansion with a red door, slightly ajar and opening onto a red and white tile floor. Having a penchant for doors, I oohed and aahed until Bernie said, "You really want this, don't you?"

We chatted with the British artist and told her that we would like the painting. All was fine until we handed her our credit card.

"I'm so sorry, but I don't take a credit card," she said politely in her British accent.

"Oh, my," Bernie replied. "Well, we don't have enough cash on hand, so where is the closest ATM?"

With a shy discomfort, the lady whispered, "I'm afraid it's at the bottom of the mountain."

"Well," Bernie said with dismay as he looked at me. "I guess we better get going."

"Oh," the artist hesitantly added, "I must tell you that I need to leave in about thirty minutes."

Oh là là!

Bernie grabbed my hand, and we ran **all** the way down the back side of *Montmartre* to the ATM and **all** the way back up to pay her. Steps, steps, steps! In our absence, at Bernie's hint of something missing in the painting, she had added a petit white poodle peaking around the red door. Bernie was delighted because he's a huge dog-lover. The painting graces the front entrance of my condo to this day.

Another special memory happened on an evening walk for coffee. We kept noticing people dressed all in white. I said to Bernie, "Someone must be getting married. How come all of these people are dressed in white?"

Dîner en Blanc in the *Place des Vosges*

As we walked closer to *La Place des Vosges*, we continued to see more and more people wearing white. Then suddenly, there was a massive rush of folks from every direction—all dressed in white at what was evidently an appointed time. Some were carrying picnic baskets, tables, chairs; others had tablecloths, candles, wine, you name it. By the time we got inside the square, line after line of white-clad mobs were encroaching on the park. Some had already set up their wares. Rows and rows of tables were elegantly and distinctively arranged. Groups of friends had obviously done a great deal of pre-planning. There was eventually no room for us, and we had to get out of the park to make way for the diners. We discovered later that this phenomenon has been going on in Paris for several years and is called *Dîner en Blanc* or Dinner in White. It was started by a Parisian businessman who was hosting a small party in one of the parks. He had invited people who did not know each another, and he had cleverly suggested that they all dress in white for easy recognition. This has turned into a yearly Parisian mania that has spread to include an elite group numbering in the thousands. It's a huge secret as to when and where the dinner will be held each summer, known only to those who have been invited into the exclusive ranks. This has been picked up by other large cities throughout the world. If you're interested in reading more about it, google *http://paris.dinerenblanc.info/about.*

Another favorite outing was the time we attended a live performance of the Broadway play *Mamma Mia* in one of Paris' classic old theatres. The musical has run continuously for years, and the performances are always sold out! It was, of course, all in French, but not a problem, since music is the universal language. We were familiar with the songs and knew the storyline well. The production had a delightful extra dose of sexy French sizzle in the choreography and costuming. We might well have been the only Americans in the audience. The patrons were rowdy, stood during much of the performance, danced in the aisles, and sang boisterously along with every song. It was a hoot. Check it out on line. Tickets should be fairly easy to get and relatively inexpensive.

Throughout our trips, Bernie has taken me repeatedly to his birthplace and then to the home where he grew up and played as a child. His mother was the concierge for a lovely apartment building in the classy 16th *arrondissement*. They lived in the basement, and Bernie's small bed was under the water heater! His best friend at ages seven and eight was another lad named Bernard. They used to skate up and down the streets, whipping around light poles, which are still there, and mischievously jumping onto the back of the old buses for a cheap ride. As you might imagine, the first time showing me his early life was very emotional. It filled in so many blanks because I had an eye-witness account of his often-shared stories. Almost every trip, we have gone back to his neighborhood, a dose of warm reminiscence for Bernie.

One of Bernie's most surprising memories was finding information on his great uncle, Général Gouraud, in the Army Museum at *Les Invalides*—quite by chance. Général Gouraud (on his mother's side) was the commanding general of the Equatorial forces in Africa. As we were meandering through the museum aisles, we noticed a large copper statue of an eagle. We stopped to read about it, and, *oh là là*, it belonged to his great uncle! He had captured this statue from the Germans in WWI. The general was also the magistrate of Paris for a time. Later, we located *La Place du Général Gouraud* in the 8th *arrondissement*. Ask me if we have a few pictures! (And in 2016, much to Bernie's delight, we found the general's statue in a little park near *Les Invalides*.)

Another Bernie-favorite moment was discovering, again by chance, the church where he was baptized, *L'Eglise Saint-Amboise* in the 11th *arrondissement*. (This is very near where Bernie was born and near the site of the *Charlie Hebdo* tragedy.) Whenever we run across a new church as we're strolling, we usually go inside. On this particular day, Bernie had a strange feeling that he had been here before. He met with the priest for quite a while in the apse of the massive cathedral and discovered that he had indeed been baptized in this church. What a moment!

Our favorite *Métro* stop is Line 12 at *La Place de la Concorde* which we use frequently. Coming from Line 1 and walking through the tunnels to Line

12, we round a corner and suddenly a beautiful station comes into view. It is decorated in small blue and white square tiles, each containing a letter of the alphabet or a punctuation mark. At first, the effect appears to be gibberish, but actually is the "Declaration of the Rights of Man" dating from the French Revolution in 1789. It is, of course, in French and striking to behold. People stop, stare, begin to read, and take lots of selfies!

I can't forget the romantic café, *La Flore en l'Ile* located on *Ile Saint-Louis*. For our nightly after-dinner outing if the weather is not too hot, this is my spot. Not only are the views of the *Seine* and *Notre Dame* breathtaking, but the people-watching is fascinating—it sits next to a pedestrian bridge full of musicians and other bizarre entertainers. And the *chocolat chaud* is some of the best. The presentation consists of warm, melted dark chocolate and hot milk served in separate small, silver pitchers which I pour and mix myself. If that's not enough, the waiters bring two divine chocolate truffles— just for being patrons—no extra charge! It's the perfect end to a Parisian day and only a ten-minute walk from our apartment.

After a busy day in traffic and crowds, we are drawn to a quaint park at the end of *Ile Saint- Louis* referred to as "The Point." It's a bucolic spot with tall trees and a few benches where we can see out across the river, wave to the tourist boats, and take in the Parisians down below enjoying picnics with friends. Always breezy, it's a perfect spot to watch day drift into night through the lens of twilight.

I cannot forget to highlight *Au Bouquet Saint-Paul*. This little neighborhood dive known to very few folks who visit Paris is right below our apartment and holds special charm for us. It's our go-to spot when we're tired, or it's raining, or we don't want expensive dining. Each year, we get to know all the work staff, and they, us. It's not fine dining, but tasty enough, and the price is right. It feels like home to us.

I'm quite sure that if you asked **a** hundred people, "What's your favorite area in Paris?" you would likely get a hundred different answers. Perhaps it's where they first stayed, or where their tour guide has taken them; maybe it's their favorite restaurant, shopping street, or museum. For us, we've had precious time now over eleven years to carefully examine **many** areas in Paris. At the very top of our favorites list is *Le Marais* with its character, historic charm, museums, modern chic, great boutiques, funny attire, and beautiful churches. Home to many everyday Parisians, it exudes a convivial spirit and energy that never disappoints. We will give you all the ritzy, posh spots in Paris and take *Le Marais* hands down anytime.

We hope you've enjoyed this mishmash of some of our favorites. After visiting Paris, you will claim your own, and we can only hope that **Bernie's Paris** has given you some great suggestions!

CHAPTER 17

The Worst Trip Ever

Le Voyage de l'enfer

~~~

A journey is a fragment of Hell.

– MOHAMED

To THINK THAT WE WOULD be lucky enough to have had eleven perfect jaunts to Paris without any hiccups would feel unnatural and certainly unbelievable. So this chapter is the needed dose of reality to right any misconceptions that we somehow live in a Pollyanna bubble.

Our tale of love and travel took on an entirely new dimension as we slogged through our one terrible trip—"the worst trip ever" or as the French title translates, "the trip from Hell." I'm not exaggerating or fabricating one word of what I'm about to share. Horrific then and funny now, I hope you find it compelling. We certainly did! It's a miracle that we ever returned to Paris, but we did. **And** we're glad we did. We're survivors and damn proud of it.

Every drama has a point of view and a storyteller. In this chapter, that is *moi*. Bernie might tell the story a little differently from a man's perspective, but the basics would be the same. We still laugh about how this one crazy trip beat us up at every turn!

SOME BAD OMENS

It was May of 2009. Bernie discovered that he had a severe urinary tract infection about two days before it was time to leave. The doctor did all the tests, and, without lab results, prescribed an antibiotic based on his best guess. He told Bernie to call him before leaving the country to make sure he had the correct medicine. To say that Bernie was not his best self is an understatement. To say that I was uneasy and worried is putting it lightly. However, we left in good faith that all would be well. That was our first mistake.

On the morning of departure, we did our usual final task of turning off the water at my house. The turn-off valve was in the front yard under the water meter cover. On that cool, clear May morning, Bernie arrived early, wearing his traveling outfit of light-colored Dockers and sport shirt. When he removed the cover on the manhole, he found the valve totally buried in mud, something which had never happened before. Bernie tried to find the valve, digging down with his bare hands in mud up to his elbows. I was freaking out and ran to grab a bucket of water, some towels, and something to dig with. He got on his hands and knees (in his very nice beige Dockers) and finally found the valve. He washed off in the bucket as best he could, but what a messy beginning for our sixteen hours to Paris!

As all of this was happening, a neighbor crossed the street to say goodbye. Her observation to me in her sweet, Southern Baptist vocabulary was that "the devil had gotten into our trip." Having no idea how much a prophet she would be, she even said a short prayer for our safe travels. Bernie and I should have both dropped to our knees right then!

Now running a little late, we rushed to catch the first leg of our trip out of the Huntsville airport. Bernie was totally not himself—nervous, agitated, complaining of joint pain in his hands and wrists, and aching all over. "It must be his rheumatoid arthritis," I thought to myself, and I dismissed it as that. But as the hours clicked by, he became more and more rattled and disoriented. By the time we arrived in Newark, the armpit of the flying world, I was scared.

We had a five-hour layover and were sitting in the first class waiting lounge of our airline when I began to nag Bernie (for the third time) that he should call his doctor. Remember our speeds? Bernie's rule is, "Why do something right away when you can put it off until the last minute?"

"Bernie!" I said with great irritation, "it's already four o'clock, and you still haven't called the doctor."

"Linda, would you please just let me handle this?" Bernie snapped with his usual exasperation.

"Well, how long are you going to wait? We need to find out if you're on the right medicine before it gets any later. You're acting crazy. And I'm really getting worried!" I snipped back, knowing my comments would probably make matters worse.

"Damnit it, Linda, you always have to push me. Okay, okay!! I'm calling the doctor right now."

The news was not good. The medicine Bernie had was **not** what he needed to beat the UTI. Bernie told the doctor about his symptoms, and they decided he must be having an allergic reaction to the sulfa drug. The doctor told Bernie that he had called in a new prescription to a pharmacy located in the Newark airport. He told us to immediately find the pharmacy and get Bernie started on the new drug. That sounds relatively easy, doesn't it? Well, the next two hours were pure hell.

We left the waiting room together and began asking airport officials where the pharmacy was, only to be told that there was no pharmacy on the premises! Finally, we found someone who said there was a pharmacy in another concourse accessible only by the airport train. We had already checked our bags and gone through security. In order to get back out of security and access another concourse was no easy process. We located an official who helped us get special passes to exit the secure area. (The seconds were ticking.) When we meandered around and finally found the exit, Bernie suddenly could not find the pass that the airport official had just given him! (I'm now more than freaking out.) He said he must have dropped it when he was fumbling with his passport. I looked at him and bluntly said, "You go back to the waiting area, and I will go get the prescription."

With my pass in hand, I set out to find the train. I was running now as I looked at my watch. It was about five-thirty; and our boarding time was six-thirty with a seven o'clock departure—in the original concourse, opposite the one I was trying to find.

I rode the train, ran down the escalator, and onto the new concourse, looking frantically for the pharmacy. Finally, I spotted it, raced up to the counter, and broke in line, saying that I had an emergency. The pharmacist was expecting me and was very helpful, getting me taken care of as fast as she could. I paid, grabbed the sack with the new antibiotic, and started the reverse trek across the airport. By the time I got back to our concourse, I was racing toward security, only to see Bernie walking toward me with a despondent look on his face. I asked what he was doing, and he frantically told me that he had lost his passport! He thought it was somewhere back where we had gotten the special passes. I told him he simply had to find it, and I headed for security—again. I had one small carry-on which I had been pulling this entire time. I got through security, realizing that it was almost time to board our flight for Paris. As I was running to the gate, I realized that I had left my carry-on back at security. I raced back and miraculously saw my bag just sitting off to the side. (It had to be my neighbor's prayer!) I hauled it back to the gate and rushed up to the check-in counter to explain what had happened to Bernie. I begged them to hold off and not close the door, pleading that I was sure Bernie would show up soon. I asked almost in tears, "What will happen if he can't find his passport?"

"We're so sorry, *madame*," the attendant said very politely, "but no passport means no ID which means no flight!"

"Where can he go to get a new passport?" I asked.

The reply almost took me to my knees.

"You will have to ride a commuter train in the morning to Philadelphia!"

Oh, my God!!

By this time, I was beginning to unravel, with thoughts of all the plans we'd made dissolving before my eyes. I continued to beg the airline to hold the door open and give us just a little more time. They were super nice, said they would not charge us for another ticket in the morning (which was amazing), but were adamant that the plane would have to depart on time that evening. Totally defeated, I went over to one of the waiting area seats, sat down, put my hands over my face, and began to sob. A female attendant came over to comfort me, but what could she do?

All of a sudden, I looked up through my tears and saw Bernie in the distance, loping down the long hall toward the gate. I stood up and started screaming, "Run, Bernie, run! Run! Run!"

Bernie is not one to hurry (as you know by now), and he was sick. But it seemed to me he was in slow motion. I rushed up to him and said, "Did you find your passport?"

He replied sheepishly, "It was in my pocket all the time."

Holy Crap! How could this be happening? I grabbed his hand, and we ran on the plane, collapsing in our seats, most certainly, the last people to board. I called my dear friend who had taken us to the airport and said, "You won't believe what just happened!" In my gut, I knew that we were in for a dreadful trip.

The Middle – Another Omen

With the correct antibiotic, Bernie became his usual self again pretty quickly, and we had a few enjoyable weeks in our Paris apartment. **But** the stage was already set for chaos even before we left home. Somehow, there had been a glitch in communication between Bernie and our landlady, who scheduled new renters into the apartment right in the middle of our visit. We already knew we had to vacate and started preparing for a trip to the Loire Valley to stay in our landlady's home. Though a bit inconvenient, we accepted the situation, thinking we would have a great time. We packed up all our extra possessions that weren't making the side trip and put them in storage in the cellar of our apartment building. Unbelievable! It was like something from the middle ages—musty, full of spider webs, and overall creepy. I told Bernie, "I hope everything won't mildew while we're gone!"

He, of course, said that I was crazy to worry about that. Hmmm.

Our friend and landlady, Marion, accompanied us on our departure. We rode the bus to the train station at *Montparnasse* and caught the *TGV* (high-speed train) initially, then transferred to a small, one-car, commuter train to

Saumur. The train car had seats for maybe forty people, and there were probably a hundred people on the train—standing, balancing suitcases, bicycles, baby strollers, backpacks, musical instruments, and all manner of other interesting "stuff." We were part of the unfortunate ones standing, until the car began to empty at each little village. Finally, we arrived at another small town where we got into our landlady's car for the ride to her home in *Loudun*. She drove like a maniac, as expressed by Bernie, and smoked incessantly, much to my dismay— not a good prescription for my terrible head cold. However, to her great credit, she had done everything possible to make us feel welcome and cooked us a love-ly dinner of veal cutlets, white asparagus, cheese, strawberries topped with pep-per (!) and mashed rhubarb. Yep, we were definitely in France. Then café only at the end. We wanted it with dessert, but she was emphatic about *après* (after)

Her country home was majestic in its own way. Half of the house was three hundred years old; the other half, a hundred and fifty years old. There was a bordering back wall from the eleventh century, all that remained of a castle. The property had been inhabited over the years by wealthy landowners. The gardens and swimming pool were lovely and filled with roses, calla lilies, and ivy. Our internet hook-up was a very slow phone line, a far cry from what we were used to. Transmitting my blog almost drove me crazy.

The smell of cigarette smoke inside the house from years and years of con-sumption was overpowering, but Marion had recently painted our bedroom for a fresh, clean scent. We made the best of it and truly did appreciate all of her efforts at hospitality. She arranged for our use of a van which belonged to the town pharmacist, took us to the *boucherie* (meat store), the *boulangerie* (bread store), the large *supermarché* for groceries, and made sure we knew where to buy diesel or *Gazoil*. On the first night, we had only a sink with cold water—no shower or tub; and the main toilet, a long walk down the hall, stopped working. Quick to the rescue, Marion got a plumber out early the next morning before she left on travel, giving us the house to ourselves. In her absence, we had use of her large, tiled bathroom with a shower, tub, and two sinks. We thought for certain we were in great shape. That was our second mistake.

Our hope was to have the time of our lives visiting the fabulous chateaus in the Loire Valley, and we planned to hit the trail the next day in search of as many as we could find. Our first evening, we ate at the one nice hotel downtown and discovered cuisine like a starred Parisian restaurant!

The weather was summer-sunny, and we had a few happy days of touring chateaus, winding along French country roads and eating some interesting meals. However, the shoe dropped on Sunday. We toured three different chateaus in three different little towns: *Ussé, Langeais,* and *Azay-le-Rideau.* We packed a typical French picnic lunch consisting of, what else, but a ham sandwich. The chateau at *Ussé* was by far the most outstanding of the three and was the inspiration for the legend of Sleeping Beauty. One of the towers in the castle was accessible to the very top, including the attic full of interesting *brocante* (junk, bric-a-brac) dating back hundreds of years. This chateau was beautifully furnished with period statues dressed in appropriate fashion. It also had a lovely chapel and fabulous riding stables for which it was known. *Très bien!*

All day, we had been looking forward to our dinner at *Château de Marçay*—reservations already made for seven-thirty in the evening. We had dressed up a little in anticipation of dining at this four-star resort hotel just outside *Chinon*. It is famous in the area and gorgeous. About four-thirty as we were pulling into the last chateau, Bernie got out of the car, slammed the door shut, and said with a calm, matter-of-fact certainty, "I am having a kidney stone attack!"

I was shocked, and that scared sensation hit me again. Bernie had had kidney stones twice before, so he knew exactly what was happening. We rushed through the chateau, hoping maybe that he was wrong. We got back in the car; I decided to drive as Bernie was in obvious pain.

As we approached the turn to go to our dinner, Bernie said with a tinge of panic in his voice,

"I need to get to the hospital—**now!**"

So, off I sped to get us safely back to *Loudun* and find the emergency room or *urgence* of the hospital on a Sunday afternoon at six o'clock. I drove around three times and kept missing the turn, but finally we pulled into the

ER. Immediately, they took Bernie back to an examination room after a now-comical discussion of describing a kidney stone in part English/part French. By this time, Bernie was doubled over in horrible pain, which he described as a man's labor pain. They hooked him up quickly to an IV and started pain medicine. Then they did an X-ray and ultrasound and confirmed that he indeed did have a kidney stone. *Oh là là!*

While all of this was going on, I raced back to the apartment, changed clothes, ate a sandwich and turned on all the lights. I was giving serious thought to the reality that I might be staying alone in this three-story, seventeen-room house. Thank God I had paid attention to keys, car keys, gate locks, and garage doors—so much to lock and unlock. When I got back to the hospital, Bernie was surprisingly feeling much better and was being dismissed to come home for the night. Thank goodness for his excellent French as he negotiated the financial details at the hospital. The bill was €103 or about $135. Not bad for an ER visit, IV, pain medicine, X-ray, and ultrasound. His medication was €9. He had no problems during the night, though I was holding my breath.

We decided that the next day, Monday, would be a mostly stay-at-home day. Bernie needed to rest, and we debated the wisdom of walking to that great hotel for lunch downtown. We decided to drive the car instead. Bad decision! There was a tight corner, partially blocked due to road work. To clear it, I had to swing way out, and I grazed the curb. On impact, we heard a loud *sssssss* sound and knew immediately that the tire had gone flat!

Bernie is a genius and can do anything, kidney stones and all. He changed the tire on the *Citroën*, figuring out that the spare was **underneath** the car in complicated fashion. Then we were off to the tire store. We hoped that the jolt of hitting the curb at precisely the right angle (I was only going ten miles per hour) simply broke the seal and that the repair would be easy and inexpensive. Otherwise, we would be looking at a new tire—which, of course, we had to buy. After all four tires were balanced, the grand total was $400! The restaurant we were going to for lunch which started the whole fiasco was closed on Mondays, so we went back to the house for the proverbial ham sandwich! I again assure you that I am not fabricating any of this.

A bigger dose of real life continued to step on our fairy tale, as Bernie's fever shot up to almost 102° late in the evening. We went back to the hospital. The final end result: Bernie had a kidney and bladder infection because the stone had lodged in his urinary tract. He was scheduled for surgery the next day at a hospital in a small town called *Thuoars,* about fifteen miles away. They had a kidney specialist who would do the procedure. I would have voted to go back to Paris, but it was Bernie's call, not mine. I began in a big way to discover what it felt like to navigate by myself without knowing the language, and the sense of scared was growing larger and larger.

After waiting **all** day, an ambulance took Bernie to *Thuoars* in the late afternoon. Of course, it was too late for surgery that day. The next morning, I went back to the hospital and visited with Bernie for half the day, then drove back to *Loudun* to do laundry because Bernie needed clean underwear! I walked to the *Lavomatique* in the middle of downtown, and used the washing machine by replicating what I had always done in Paris. However, the darn dryer was another story. I even asked people off the street for assistance, and they didn't know how to make it work either! I had no choice but to walk the heavy load up the steep hill to Marion's house. I deliberated over how to dry the wet clothes and finally decided to hang them on the long stairway banister. To my surprise, that decision, which I thought so clever, left a prominent brown stripe from the wood stain across all of our clothes! Fatigued, dejected, and starving, I ate dinner at the nice hotel all alone that night about eight o'clock. I was a pretty sad version of myself.

Things to remember, ladies, when you're traveling with your man—pay attention, pay attention, pay attention. Know where everything is; know how all the electronics work; know how to get in and out of wherever you're staying; know how to drive any kind of car; and have some sense of direction. Have everyone's phone number, have insurance cards, and know the address of where you're staying. Around midnight of this desolate night, I realized that if the house caught on fire and I had to call for help, I didn't even know the address. I rummaged through some mail I found at the front door and wrote down the address for Marion's house. Thank goodness I had run a television station; it was good preparation for doing whatever crazy thing I had to do.

The next day, Bernie had surgery under general anesthetic, and the surgeon removed a kidney stone the size of a healthy green pea. It would have never passed on its own. There was no communication from anyone until hours after the surgery, much to my dismay, and I count that day as one of the most stressful I've ever had. The entire episode was total confirmation that I had to start learning some basic French. Out in the small towns, people do not speak English!

Words of encouragement come flooding in via email from friends on our blog, and I took courage and strength from those. Unfortunately, more bad news awaited us. We were told that Bernie had to have a stent inserted to allow easy passage of any additional small pieces of the kidney stone which could be lodged in his urinary tract. In about ten days, he would have to be back in the hospital in Paris to have the tube removed. Poor Bernie! He was pretty discouraged, as you can imagine, and we were both frustrated and extremely disappointed that all of our plans for a glorious week in the Loire Valley had exploded. Bernie was released from the hospital, knowing that soon we had to catch a train back to Paris. He was still in a great deal of discomfort and welcomed a few days to rest at the house back in *Loudon* before the train trip.

The hospital experience was very interesting, and I suppose a first-hand look at socialized medicine. Just a few observations which you might find interesting. There was no cafeteria. A family member or friend had to reserve a meal for €8 early in the morning. The food was prepared elsewhere, and for the most part was not so great. The best part for Bernie was a huge bowl of coffee for breakfast; that's correct—a bowl. He remembered this from his childhood with fondness.

There was not an ombudsman to work with folks like me who didn't know the procedures, much less the language. (This was probably typical of a small hospital in a small town.) However, I did find a very kind lady in admissions who had a computer that translated English to French and *vice versa*.

Television usage was paid for by the hours viewed, and the phone, by the number of calls made. Everything was very clean and constantly being disinfected, a soothing comfort amid the confusion. The nurses were direct, efficient, and fast, but with little bedside manner, and they tolerated no back-talk from the patient! "Do what you're told and don't ask questions" was the message. There were no private rooms, and there was no curtain or partition to separate Bernie from his roommate or his roommate's family. The regulations we have in the States on privacy were non-existent here. We saw and heard everything from both patient and doctors.

So, you can decide how this sounds. I saw good and bad. The best thing was the surgeon himself who had a great bedside manner. Bernie asked him for an estimate of the cost, and the doctor chortled out, "I don't have a clue. The *société* will take care of it."

Bernie was very ready for his release, but then we had to figure out how to get the follow-up procedure and care scheduled in Paris without a personal physician. We feared it would be tedious even at the American Hospital in Paris and gave some thought to requesting assistance from the United States Embassy. Thank goodness, that turned out to be unnecessary.

When we returned to *Loudun*, it was a gorgeous day, and we sat outside in the city hall park across the street from Marion's house—watching, would you believe, weddings. It was seventy degrees with royal blue skies and a soft breeze. The sunshine and fresh air felt wonderful to Bernie. There were three weddings that afternoon—our source of entertainment and distraction from such a trying week. The first was at two o'clock and appeared to be the *bourgeois* elite of the city. It started with a civil ceremony at the court house followed by a parade through the streets to the church, amid a chorus of wonderful church bells. The ladies were French chic in big hats, gloves, and designer dresses, and the bride's dress was gorgeous. The three o'clock wedding appeared to be a notch down as far as attire, and then the wedding at four was even more mundane, conducted in blue jeans. After each wedding, the decorated cars paraded through town with horns blaring. It was an easy, relaxing way to spend the afternoon, and we needed that!!

Are you positive by now that I'm exaggerating this tale? Is it beginning to sound over-the-top ridiculous, melodramatic, or something out of the movies? I understand. However, be assured that it all happened in real time to two frustrated folks.

We left *Loudun* the next day for the train ride to Paris with our lunches packed and some concern about bathroom issues for poor Bernie, who still had an artificial tube stuck in his privates. The landlady had returned home and assured us as we were leaving that there would be no one on the train. Wrong! Crowded like crazy. We had two small suitcases, a big tote bag, a heavy backpack, and Bernie's computer case. We, like everyone else, looked like traveling gypsies. Train travel means constant steps and a mad scramble to find the right train, right seats, and a place to store your luggage. The first train was to be a thirty-minute ride; however, there was a problem with the track, and we were stopped for a twenty-minute delay. Given that we had a seven-minute layover for our change. . . well, you do the math. Alas, not to worry. They held the *TGV* to Paris and told us we had a very short time to make *la correspondance*. It was like ants at a picnic; thank God for Bernie's good instincts. Somehow he landed us on the right train, and we settled in to eat, you guessed it, our ham sandwiches!

We got back to Paris, switched from the train to a bus which took us back to our neighborhood. We arrived with smiling faces to find our wonderful CLEAN apartment in great shape. Then we began the arduous task of unpacking. Remember, we had left many of our belongings stored in the musty, dusty cellar of this sixteenth century building, referred to politely as *le cave* in French. We had planned a system to unpack a little at a time and carry everything up the sixty steps in tote bags, so as not to kill ourselves. Poor Bernie! I did the lion's share while he was trying to get all the electronics to work. Our computer was not recognizing the router or the internet, and I dreaded being stuck back on the damnable European keyboard once again.

It was about seven o'clock before we began to see daylight with the unpacking, and after quick showers, we were more than ready for dinner. We closed the door to our apartment, and as I always do when I am not taking my purse, I looked at Bernie and asked, "You do have the key, don't you?"

He replied with his usual frustration, "Yes, I do." (You know where this is going.)

As soon as we started down the first steps, he stopped, and with a strange sound in his voice, exclaimed, "You know what, I **don't** have the key!"

Well, my friends, the world ended for a few seconds. Our landlady was back in *Loudun,* and her phone number was inside on the computer along with any other contact information. So there we sat on the steps, so tired we could hardly move—Bernie with his tube, both of us beaten up mentally after the week that we'd had, starving, and thinking how it would feel to sleep in a hotel for the night with nothing but the clothes on our backs.

We did not have many good options. Bernie wanted to leap across a ten-foot-wide space between the landing and an open window in our apartment. He said, "I think I can make it!"

And I said in frantic response, "If you don't, you'll die right in front of me!" There was a brick-laden courtyard about forty feet below. Then I suggested we go across the street to the *pompiers,* the firemen, and he said they wouldn't help us. (I still grind at him about this one because I know they would have come with a ladder and crawled across to the open window!) But, being so politely French, Bernie didn't want to bother them! Arg!

Then I suggested that we go to the apartment above us to see if our neighbors had a ladder. The young couple upstairs who spoke great English did not have a ladder but did make it their mission to help two very distressed Americans. (They were Frank and Vinciane, whom we didn't know at that time.) Frank had a friend who was a locksmith. He called to get his advice and was told that there was only about a 30% chance he could get in easily for a fee of €150. Otherwise, to break in and replace an elaborate, high security lock would be **very expensive**! While we waited on the locksmith to journey forty-five minutes across Paris at eight o'clock at night, the neighbor invited us up for a glass of wine (which Bernie was forbidden to drink—it was killing him!) and to meet his wife and baby. For half an hour, we sat and watched a very hyperactive toddler. It was surreal! Finally, the locksmith arrived and, you guessed it, could not do the easy fix. He said that they would go purchase the correct lock and return in an hour.

Bernie took one look at me and said, "You've got to have some food!"

Frank walked us to a nearby bistro for the best pork and mashed potatoes I've ever eaten. We stopped at the ATM on the way back to get enough cash to pay the locksmith. Long story short, it cost us €800 or $1,000 to put in the new lock.

The money really didn't matter. We could get back inside the apartment and try to have a normal night and a good rest. As we were turning out the lights, I told Bernie to set the alarm, which always upsets him. He prides himself on being able to wake up at whatever appointed time—yes, a carry-over from his Boy Scout and Army days. I said that, given our luck of late, I didn't want to chance it and miss my nail appointment for ten o'clock the next morning. We have our priorities, after all!

I do hope this part of the saga has made you chuckle a bit. I was beginning to agree with my sweet neighbor at home who had insisted that the Devil had gotten into our trip!

Bernie's outpatient procedure went well a few days later. They removed the tube with no problems, which eliminated his pain and the lovely process of peeing into a big Pepsi liter bottle! A tiny piece of stone remained, but the doctor did not want to pulverize it, as he said that might cause more problems. He thought it had moved some and might pass on its own. Bernie was also clear of any infection, and he was elated that he could have a moderate amount of red wine!! Our life settled back into a degree of normalcy, and we managed to have some fun weeks in Paris during the rest of our stay. But we hadn't escaped our dark cloud just yet.

THE GRAND FINALE

It was somehow appropriate and not surprising that our departing leg of this trip from Hell should be fraught with trauma. Keep laughing because what I'm about to tell you is beyond ridiculous.

We arrived in New York City at Newark Airport about two-thirty in the afternoon to catch a connection at five o'clock. The flight was delayed, and I noticed a rowdy bunch of folks in the waiting area. At that time, I didn't understand the significance. We finally boarded the plane after an hour's wait, and we immediately saw that we were in for a bad time. Our body clocks read two o'clock in the morning, and our plan had been to sleep for most of this flight. Little by little, we figured out that the rowdy group of passengers on this very small commuter plane were all members of a baseball team going to play a championship game in Cincinnati. They were yelling row to row, front to back, telling obscene jokes, singing, intoxicated, and pretty much taking over the plane. These were grown men in their thirties and forties, but the scene played out like a high school locker room.

Suddenly the pilot came over the intercom and told us that we were number twenty-two for take-off! Welcome to the Newark airport in the late afternoon. So we tried to settle in, close our eyes, and go to sleep. With all the shouting, laughing, and other commotion, that was not going to be easy. I rang the attendant bell, explaining that we were on Paris time and really needed to sleep. We asked the flight attendant to help us out by telling these rowdy guys to settle down. She said she would. An hour and a half went by, and we still had not taken off. The locker room antics continued. Finally, the pilot lifted the requirement that everyone stay seated so that we could use the restroom. Here's where the story gets really raunchy. These baseball guys started commenting on each person's bathroom functions as to performance, stance, and size of body parts. I was so disgusted that I wouldn't even get out of my seat. Bernie was seething.

Calm, easy-going Bernie rarely gets rattled or shows his colors. However, the environment was so offensive that he undid his seatbelt, got up, went to the front, and asked the flight attendant, "When are you going to make these guys shut up?"

He came back to his seat, thinking surely we would take off soon.

After another fifteen minutes, we noticed that the plane was turning around and taxiing back to the gate. What the heck? No one understood what was happening as the plane stopped and locked into the jet way. Suddenly, the cabin door opened, and several serious-looking men entered and came right up to our seats. They looked at Bernie and asked if he was Bernard Verdier. Standing up, he said, "Yes, I am!"

"Come with us," they said in serious, gruff voices.

I jumped up and said, "Well, if he is going, so am I!"

As soon as we were off the plane and standing in the jet way, Bernie was under verbal assault by the armed officials, who accused him of harassing the flight attendant! I interrupted their rude comments and went into a screaming tirade about what a good man Bernie was, a lieutenant colonel in the United States Army for twenty-two years who had never hurt anyone, yadda, yadda, yadda. Then I told them what had **really** been going on inside the airplane **in great detail**. Their eyes widened at some of what I described. I threw in the "sexual harassment" phrase. The Delta supervisor, a female who was also present, said that she was going back on the plane and talk with other passengers. In about ten minutes, she returned with an apology to Bernie, saying that others had confirmed our tale of horrors.

Would you believe that they cancelled our flight because the pilot's allotted flying time had expired! We had to spend the night in New Jersey and catch a six o'clock flight the next morning. I made a serious attempt to get some retribution from the airlines for their rude treatment of Bernie, but that was a futile exercise, netting money only for the lawyers.

And so this worst trip ever finally came to a bizarre end in perfect synchronization with its beginning and middle. Hopefully, we will never again face anything to compare with this nightmare. Looking back five years, we're pretty amazed that we survived it, but glad that everything that could go wrong happened in one unpleasant sweep of events.

There's always a silver lining: I have the best cocktail party stories of anyone. This tale of truth always draws a big crowd. I have a good friend who coyly says, "Just tell the truth because no one will ever believe you!"

CHAPTER 18

The Annual Goodbye at Pont Marie

L'Aurevoir annuel au Pont Marie

Paris is a hard place to leave....

– WILLA CATHER

ON THE LAST WEEK OF each year's visit, I grow a tight knot in my throat, a sluggishness in my gait like having weights in my shoes, and a dread of the final few days. It's almost like waiting for a funeral. Paris is not my hometown, but it has become a piece of me. And I get really sad as departure time nears. It hits Bernie even harder.

I start emptying the refrigerator, using up everything we possibly can, which means no more eating out and no more trips to the market or grocery store. Bernie goes through all the memorabilia he has meticulously collected with absolute intent of needing, only to throw it all away as he prepares to pack.

A day or so before we leave, we take advantage of *La Poste,* the national government postal service. It's one of the institutions which run very efficiently in Paris. We use their flat-rate box to ship home heavier purchases, shoes, or books to help reduce our suitcase weight. We buy the ten-kilo box, which holds about twenty-two pounds, and it arrives in America shortly after we do.

We pull out dusty suitcases from behind furniture, stairwells, and doors. We begin talking about departure times and setting alarms and arranging for a taxi. Then, when the final evening arrives, we have our last cup of coffee at one of our favorite spots, and take one last walk—our final *au revoir.*

None of this is done by chance. We have a goodbye spot, a farewell place that is sacred to both of us. We walk down the length of *rue St. Paul,* saying good-bye to our friend Patrick, past the Thanksgiving store, past *Méli-Mélo,* and pausing carefully at the bicycle lane crossing. We wait pensively for the double light to show us a green man, and then we cross over to the river. Slowly we caress the wall along *Quai des Célestins* with the river on our left, walking slightly uphill to the intersection at *Pont Marie.* Next, we make a left turn onto the bridge which has touched our feet more than any other. It seems only appropriate to be our final look at Paris. *Pont Marie* is known as the "bridge of lovers," and legend has it that if you kiss under it and wish for eternal love, your wish will come true.

We walk silently to the middle where other lovers are huddled. Usually, it's twilight; usually, a warm breeze caresses our cheeks. We look out across the River *Seine* to the skyline of Paris, where one bridge tumbles into another like dominos cascading into the horizon. As Kate Simon says in her book *PARIS,* "…return to the *Seine* and watch the evening sky close slowly on a last strand of daylight fading quietly, like a sigh."

Twilight view from *Pont Marie*

We both tear up; we embrace; we hold a tender kiss; we shudder our own wistful sigh. And we realize how blessed we are. Then, with coupled hands, we silently walk home. The sadness holds us for only a little while. Tomorrow is another day—a busy day of travel, tight schedules, and exhaustion.

As we pack up one more year of glorious memories, we have only one remaining thought—

"So, when's our trip next year?"

CHAPTER 19

Reflections on Personal Change

Réflexions

⟶ᒡ

Paris is a place in which we can forget ourselves,
reinvent, expunge the dead weight of our past.

– MICHAEL SIMKINS, *DETOUR DE FRANCE: AN ENGLISHMAN*
IN SEARCH OF A CONTINENTAL EDUCATION

ALL THROUGH THIS BOOK, I have alluded to how my time in Paris has changed me. That deserves some final comments.

I think it's important to state that I was a well-traveled gal before ever going to Paris. I had traveled all over the United States including Alaska and Hawaii. I had been to almost every country in Europe. I had been through the Middle Eastern country of Turkey and the old Slavic nations of Bulgaria, Rumania, Yugoslavia, and Czechoslovakia, as well as to the former Soviet Socialist Republic. I had visited such unique cities as Istanbul, Yalta, Odessa, Prague, Dubrovnik, Venice, Rome, Florence, London, Dublin, Cannes, Monte Carlo, Bruges, Lucerne, Vancouver, and Amsterdam.

My point is that I was not wide-eyed and naive the first time I saw Paris. My mind had already been opened to some of the lessons that only traveling can teach. But it is odd that Paris was the one city, the one amazing place, which I had never visited in all of my travels!

Fate, I think, saved Paris for me until I met Bernie, until I was almost in my sixties, until I had gotten past how to ride a train, change money, use strange bathrooms, eat different food, and negotiate foreign conversations. I was not overwhelmed with the peculiarities of new cultures but primed for the infusion of a new perspective to grace my persona. It has not been easy to put the changes into words, but I will try.

I have learned about small spaces and ancient buildings where people live in less than a thousand square feet. And they live quite well. Hearing my neighbors is a sign of consolation rather than irritation. I have learned to abandon excess and overabundance for a quaint contentment with having just enough. I have learned about tiny streets called *rues* where two cars can barely pass. I have learned that old doesn't mean useless; that old doesn't mean two hundred years but several centuries; that preserving the past is about how to live in the present constructively. I have learned about conservation of energy and natural resources. I have learned about fresh foods and daily trips to the market because of small freezers and lack of preservatives. France has the market on organic, producing some of the best fruits and vegetables in Europe.

I have learned to appreciate the French take on sex and body parts, not as mouth-dropping, eye-popping sins, but as simply a part of life. Women openly breast-feed babies, and little tykes pee-pee on the sidewalk in an emergency. And no one notices! Without the ever-hovering Puritan heritage, the French embrace sex with a relaxed ease which should not be deemed immoral or amoral. It's a refreshing change. They have removed the drama from sexual emphasis and fail to buy into our sexual hang-ups.

I have learned that it all starts with *"Bonjour,"* meaning that politeness opens the door to the French. Tone of voice, polite greetings, sincere apologies, attempts to speak a language that is so difficult (with a Southern Alabama accent), all count for progress in the right direction. I have learned to slow down, *sans* meetings, texts, or phone calls. I have indulged in slow, easy mornings, which usually begin no earlier than eleven o'clock. I have learned to love church bells. I have learned to stroll—something Americans do not do—in parks and down shady boulevards and across ancient bridges. I have learned to say, "Well, it's Paris" and let irritations fall by the wayside. I don't get hot and bothered anymore because a shop is not open when its posted hours say it should be. I don't get angry when the restaurants are closed on Mondays, or the hairdresser doesn't have my American hairspray in stock. I have learned to eat much later in the evening and to relish a slow dinner for two or three hours. I don't tap my foot as impatiently as I used to when the waiter doesn't bring our bill for what seems like an eternity. I have learned to eat everything on my plate so as not to offend a waiter. I have watched and listened to what seemed odd circumstances or frustrating situations and soothed myself with the endearing phrase, "It's France; it's complicated." I have learned to live with black dust and the grime of automobile exhaust which grows overnight on floors and furniture. My tendency toward being overly fussy about cleanliness has withered before my eyes. I am able to laugh and embrace a Parisian love of life.

It's been like growing a new skin with fewer wrinkles!

Wayne Dyer contends in *Manifest Your Destiny* that we get back that which we emanate. Nowhere is this truer than in Paris. I have learned to gesture, to talk with my eyes, to coo with my voice, and to let Parisians know that I love being with them—in their country, in their culture, in their hearts. I can sing out *Oh là là* with the best of them. I have embraced their cores, and nothing affects a relationship as much as being soulmates. To my surprise, they have reciprocated warmly.

In Paris, I am not out to impress anyone, including myself. I live and let live and enjoy a less stressful daily life. Few people know me, and that anonymity is freeing. It's like my body heaves a deep sigh and relaxes. I am mesmerized by the constant flow of the *Seine*. I can stand for hours and watch how the setting sun kisses the graceful arches of *Notre Dame* or the towers of *La Conciergerie* or the statues adorning *l'Hôtel de Ville*. The sparkling light is a force itself, a statement revealing the inner heart of Paris and the deep layers of its past. The language is a song to my ears—so delicate, so flowing, so lyrical. I have come to understand French more than I can speak it, and hearing the native tongue has become soothing instead of strange. Even when I don't understand the words, I still get the meaning through the tone, the gestures, and the delightful facial expressions, especially from French women.

Yes, the French can be aloof and rude; they can be arrogant and opinionated; **but** more than anything, they can also be tender. Once you latch onto this personality secret, it explains so much. They are tolerant, quiet, forgiving, restrained, especially in public. They don't look to see what's happening around them, or judge how someone is dressed, or eavesdrop on conversations. They mind their own business. They're not shocked by the drama of day-to-day life. They simply rock along with whatever life presents to them, which is a part of their stoic history. Folks are subdued in their demeanor, but that doesn't mean they don't offer help to total strangers or grab strollers on subway steps to assist a young mother. It doesn't mean they don't give up their seats to the elderly, or stop to ask if you need directions. And if they run into you by mistake, they fall over themselves with polite apologies. Men kiss men in greeting, and girlfriends walk hand in hand together down busy streets with seemingly not a care in the world. Families buy *Berthillion* ice cream together on Sunday afternoons, and elderly couples stroll affectionately, arms entwined, dressed in their best outfits of bygone fashion.

Tender, yes, tender is probably the most revealing word that captures the core of being French.

I am richer, fuller, more serendipitous, less inclined to stereotype or judge. I have been suspended in a cloud of make-believe for two glorious months of the past eleven years. I say goodbye each year with profound sadness because I feel like I'm leaving the best part of me somewhere on the subways or in the parks or along the beloved *Seine.*

What has Paris done to my relationship with Bernie? Ah, that one is even harder to express. It has made me understand his love of country, his regret over being forced to leave Paris at such an early age, and his intense desire to spend whatever time he has left with members of his French family. It has helped me understand his fierce combative method of debate, "discussion" as he calls it; his ease of savoring a glass of red wine or a glass of *Ricard*; his desire to speak to other Frenchmen in his native tongue, or to enjoy a two or three-hour evening meal without being rushed. He is never better than when in Paris, so we are never better—alive, unencumbered, and dependent on each other's time and devotion, intently knitted together almost every hour. Some might be smothered, but for us, it's the epitome of happiness. Paris is the environment which releases the best we have to offer each other. Even during the worst of circumstances, we have pressed forward.

I have learned about love—not the bed-thumping, lusty kind of our twenties and thirties, but the deeper variety—stitched in layers of friendship, trust, loyalty and kindness—which over time has soaked up the rum of life. I have learned that Paris is my healer of decisions made poorly, of romances gone wrong, of my broken spirit, my broken heart, and my loss of hope. Paris was meant for me at exactly this time in my life with exactly this man in my life. It has been the yeast for a life that was flat, the tempo for music gone silent, the spice for a chemistry that had become dormant. I owe Paris my life!

Just to be clear, I love my country, my city, my children, my grandchildren, my friends, and my neighbors; and I miss them all when I am gone. But Paris, beautiful Paris, has carved out a special *niche* in my heart. It is Bernie's Paris that I have learned to love, shared by him as a gift to me in what have become the best years of my life. It is Bernie's Paris that has given me cause to discover the best piece of myself.

Won't you come and discover Bernie's Paris and write your travel stories, with love?

Hurry! Go pack. We'll see you in the hood!

References on Paris

1. If you would like to receive our travel blogs from Paris, go to *www. lindaspalla.com* to subscribe.
2. For tours of Paris and the cooking class with Charlotte Puckett, contact Richard Nahem at *www.eyepreferparis.com*
3. For tours of Paris with a native, contact Anne Jeanne at *www. afriendinparis.com*
4. Books I have read and recommend about Paris and France:
    * *Pure* by Andrew Miller, 2012
    * *Savoir Flaire* by Polly Platt, 2000
    * *The Greater Journey by* David McCullough, 2012
    * *The Paris Wife* by Paula McClain, 2012
    * *Sarah's Key* by Tatiana de Rosnay, 2008
    * *The House I Loved* by Tatiana de Rosnay, 2012
    * *Abundance — A Novel of Marie Antoinette* by Sena Jeter Naslund, 2006
    * *How to Be Parisian Wherever You Are* by Anne Brest, Audrey Diwan, Caroline de Maigret, and Sophie Mas, 2014
    * *The Lady and the Unicorn Tapestries* by Tracy Chevalier, 2004
    * *Paris: The Novel* by Edward Rutherfurd, 2013
    * *Meet Paris Oyster* by Mireille Guiliano, 2014
    * *The Paris Effect* by Michelle Moggio, 2014
    * *The Paris Effect* by K.S.R. Burns, 2015
    * *Lovers at the Chameleon Club, Paris 1932* by Francine Prose, 2013

"SAYING GOOD-BYE TO a city is harder than breaking up with a lover. The grief and regret are more piercing because they are more complex and unmixed, changing from corner to corner, with each passing vista, each shift of the light. Breaking up with a city is unclouded by the suspicion that after the affair ends, you'll learn something about the beloved you wished you never knew. The city is as it will remain: gorgeous, unattainable, going on without you as if you'd never existed. What pain and longing the lover feels as he bids farewell to a tendril of ivy, a flower stall, the local butcher. The charming café where he meant to have coffee but never did. Magnify those feelings a thousand fold when the city is Paris. Every bridge is a pirate's plank the lover walks at his own peril, watching the twinkling *Seine* and giving serious thought to jumping and losing himself in that seductive, sparkly blackness. Every spire pierces the heart. Every alley, every smoky tabac, every fountain was killing me."

5. List of other books on Paris
   * *Paris Letters* by Janice MacLeod, 2014
   * *Hidden in Paris* by Corine Gantz, 2011
   * *A Paris Apartment: A Novel* by Michelle Gable, 2014
   * *Seven Letters from Paris: A Memoir* by Samantha Vérant, 2014
   * *The Paris Journal* by Nichole Robertson, Evan Robertson, 2014
   * *Paris, Paris: Journey into the City of Light* by David Downie, Alison Harris, Diane Johnson, 2005
   * *Paris in Love* by Nichole Robertson, 2013
   * *Almost French: Love and a New Life in Paris* by Sarah Turnbull, 2002
   * *We'll Always Have Paris: A Mother/Daughter Memoir* by Jennifer Coburn, *2014*
   * *My Paris Dream* by Kate Betts, 2015
   * *Postcards from France* by Gai Reid, 2015
6. More about *Le Viaduc des Arts http://europeforvisitors.com/paris/articles/viaduc-des-arts.htm.*

7. More about *Dîner en blanc* Google *http://paris.dinerenblanc.info/about.* "At the last minute, the location is given to thousands of friends and acquaintances who have been patiently waiting to learn the *Dîner en Blanc's* secret place. Thousands of people, dressed all in white, and conducting themselves with the greatest decorum, elegance, and etiquette, all meet for a mass "chic picnic" in a public space. Over the course of an evening, the diners enhance the function and value of their city's public space by participating in the unexpected. Beyond the spectacle and refined elegance of the dinner itself, guests are brought together from diverse backgrounds by a love of beauty and good taste. *Le Dîner en Blanc* recalls the elegance and glamour of court society, and diners engage one another knowing they are taking part in a truly magical event. There are no disruptions: no car traffic, no pedestrian traffic, except for the occasional amazed and astonished looks from passersby at the scene unfolding before them. And we, as they, wonder whether it's all not a dream…Launched with just a handful of friends by Francois Pasquier over 25 years ago, Paris' *Dîner en Blanc* now assembles nearly 15,000 people each year. The French capital's most prestigious sites have played host to it: *Le Pont des Arts,* the Eiffel Tower site, *Place Vendôm,* the *Esplanade de Notre-Dame,* the *Esplanade des Invalides, l'Avenue Champs-Elysées, Place de la Concorde* and this year's location *Le Louvre Pyramid* and the *Trocadéro Esplanade* at the same time! The Paris police tend to tolerate this 'wild'gathering, if not perhaps even wishing they could join in!"

8. Check out this recipe for *Île Flottante* from the Barefoot Contessa: *http://www.foodnetwork.com/recipes/ina-garten/ile-flottante-recipe. html?oc=linkback*

Made in the USA
Lexington, KY
20 October 2016